FROM NOTHING

IAN PRIBYL

Contact:
ian@StoppingScams.com

Editing by:
My extraordinary wife, Regina Pribyl

Cover Design by:
Diren Yardimli, *DirenYardimli.com*

Book Layout & Formatting by:
Luca Funari, *lucafunari@hotmail.com*

All concepts, training, and screenshots within this book are pulled from the 15+ hours of video training at First-Time Internet Marketing Profits™ (FIMP).

CONTENTS

This book is dedicated to you, the reader.

I hope it helps you build an internet business that provides you the same freedom and independence that mine has provided me.

INTRODUCTION

Hello there, and welcome to the "FIMP Fam!"

If that doesn't make any sense to you, I'll explain in just a moment.

"Bleh, an introduction."

I know, I know. As someone who's been known to read a book or two, I know how itchy your fingers might be right now to turn the page and get into the "good stuff."

However, **read <u>ALL</u> of this brief introduction.** It will have a critical impact on your success (or failure) following the contents of this book.

The Purpose of This Book

The purpose of this book is to help you build a profitable online business using less than $100 in startup capital.

It doesn't matter if you're brand new and know nothing about online business, or if you've "been around the block" a time or two and wasted a bunch of money on products in this industry.

It doesn't matter if you're "tech challenged" or if you're "one with technology" as much as Neo from *The Matrix*.

I'm confident you'll find this book easy-to-follow, and that it contains **everything** you need to build an internet business from scratch (OR overhaul an existing one to get it on a profitable track).

I created FIMP so that people who want to change their lives are able to without breaking the bank. The sad reality of the Internet Marketing industry is that there are several product publishers who only have one goal in mind: money. They create expensive products that claim to teach you how to make money online but instead provide out-dated/incomplete methods, only teach you how to promote their product and nothing else, or flat-out nickel and dime you by recommending a bunch of unnecessary tools and services nobody actually needs when they're just starting out.

It's a cycle that leaves people disappointed and broke, and it gives the entire industry a bad name.

I don't recommend **anything** that's unnecessary when you're just getting started. Many people find this so "against the grain" versus what they're used to seeing in this industry that many find it confusing (more on that in a moment as well).

This is Not the ONLY Path To a Profitable Online Business for < $100

I've personally never explored another path in online business that led to so much profit with so little capital investment, BUT...

They're out there and I don't want to give anyone the impression that they're not.

I can only teach from my own experiences over the last 10+ years. I don't know (nor would I ever **pretend** to know) every path to online profit using less than $100.

But what I **DO** know, beyond a shadow of a doubt, is that this book will deliver first-time success in online business if you've never experienced it before. You'll need to study and follow it closely, though.

What's taught in this book are the most time-tested and universally-accessible strategies to find success in online business without a large budget. It doesn't matter if you follow FIMP (the video training this book was derived from) or another complete system that is run by someone you trust – find **one**, stick with it until you achieve success, and experiment/combine later.

Most tactics/strategies within this industry do **NOT** combine well, and it usually takes a seasoned Internet Marketer to know what's compatible and what's not.

If you find the strategies within this book aren't for you, you're welcome to jump back into "the wild" and try your hand following other training.

Keep in mind, particularly in the dog-eat-dog world of Internet Marketing/online business/make money online/etc., that there's a 99% chance that the person you end up following is just bashing you like a piñata full of cash, bleeding a little bit more with every blow...

Even if you can't feel each strike of the bat.

"Internet Marketing" vs. "Blogging" vs. "eCommerce" vs. "Online Business" vs. "Making Money Online," Etc.

"I don't want to learn Internet Marketing, Ian. I want to learn how to blog!"

It doesn't matter if you want to build an eCommerce website, a dropshipping website, a blog, an affiliate marketing business, a lead generation business, a service-based business, or any other common form of monetization in this industry.

If you want to build ANY of those businesses, you need to learn how to market on the internet. That's why we're referred to as "Internet Marketers" and why this book often refers to these business models using the all-encompassing umbrella of "Internet Marketing."

So don't get discouraged by this term, even if it's new to you. If you're trying to build a profitable business on the internet, the skillset you need to develop is "Internet Marketing."

This Book Is a Written Companion to First-Time Internet Marketing Profits™ (FIMP)

With that said, this book is written specifically to stand very well on its own, even if you never step foot inside the 15+ hours of video training at FIMP.

If you found this book before finding FIMP, but you'd like to check it out, you can join our community, ask questions when you're stuck, and study all of the high-quality video training at *https://StoppingScams.com/FIMP/* — but don't feel obligated!

There are certainly a lot of extra perks to creating an account, and we'd love to have you! Plus, some of the step-by-step stuff is easier to follow when you're watching a video "over my shoulder."

Sometimes a book is more convenient to digest and study. Use one, or use them both! Either way, please just use them for what they're designed to do:

Help you take control of and change your life by building a profitable internet business.

"Why Aren't You Recommending the Tools Everyone Else Recommends?"

Sometimes people are a little bit confused when joining FIMP. They don't understand why I don't dig deeply into landing page software, email marketing software, premium themes & plugins, etc.

Trust me — those elements and recommendations aren't present **intentionally**.

In 99% of cases, they're just flat-out unnecessary for where you're at in your business. People recommend them so commonly in this industry because every purchase you make through their link earns them an affiliate commission.

By recommending a bunch of stuff you don't need (even though they most often recommend it under the guise that it's required), they're boosting the lifetime value (LTV) of their subscriber — that's you!

And it comes at your expense.

I don't do that at FIMP or within this book. Are many of those tools helpful? Yes, but not until you have consistent traffic that makes them worth the investment.

If you're spending thousands of dollars on paid advertising from the get-go, you need to invest in these tools from day one. But if you're cash-strapped and making up for your lack of startup capital using "elbow grease," like this book and FIMP's video course teaches, **you don't need premium tools until <u>at least</u> several months from now.**

So, put your wallet away and don't write off this book or FIMP just because we're the "odd man out" for not taking you for every dime possible.

I'm Not Going to Waste Your Time With a Flashy "About Me"

IIIIIIIIIIIIIIIIIIIIIIIIIIIIIIIIIIIIIIIIIIIIIIIIIIIIIIIIIIIIIIIIIIIIIIIIIIIIIIIIIIIIIIIIIIIIIIIIIIIIIIIII

I'm not trying to dazzle or impress you.

If gurus flashing Lamborghinis while recording a sales video in a mansion they rented for the day is a prerequisite for you to trust me, you're going to be disappointed.

I'll talk a little bit about how I got my start online (I began this journey with **nothing**), why I was initially attracted to internet business, and I'll even share a little bit about my income over the years within this book.

I'd prefer to be judged by my body of work: the success stories and testimonials created within the FIMP community, and the depth of Internet Marketing expertise I demonstrate within these pages and the 15+ hours of video training at FIMP.

If you don't trust me because I'm not flashing rapidly-depreciating financial assets on camera, send me an email at *ian@stoppingscams.com* and I'll refund your purchase price of this book.

Now Go Forth and Prosper ☺

I sincerely appreciate you taking a few minutes to read this introduction.

You've now properly "set the stage" and set yourself up for success while studying the rest of the book.

Take a deep breath whenever you feel overwhelmed, be kind and forgiving to yourself as you stumble (mistakes are how we learn!), and feel free to connect with me and the rest of the FIMP community online if you need a hand along the way.

Let your suppressed, itchy fingers fly!

Not **THAT** one.

Oh just turn the page already.

And enjoy ☺

Chapter 1: The ONLY Way Anyone Gets Rich Online

If you're reading this book, you're probably interested in building an online business.

Well, let me tell you this now: **VERY** few people who attempt to strike it rich online actually succeed. Want to know what the main difference is between successful internet business owners and the mass graves of unsuccessful "wannabes?"

Read on to find out.

1.1 How to Use This Book to Build a Five to Six Figure Internet Business

Before we get deep into concepts and strategies, let me tell you first how to use this book to change your life and build a five to six figure-a-year internet business.

My internet business produces five figures a month. I haven't sustainably broken six figures a month, but I *have* made six figures in total revenue a handful of times in e-commerce. My goal is to achieve that in internet business by the next year or two.

If your early stage goal is to replace a four-figure salary, it's definitely achievable in this industry if approached the right way.

So, how do you use this book to do that? **The first step is to read chapters 1 and 2 in their entirety**, and here's why:

Chapter 1 describes how to make the most out of this book and breaks down Internet Marketing into its core components. Once these concepts are understood, the entire process is much less overwhelming.

Chapter 2 discusses what I've found to be the two strongest determining factors to success in this industry: realistic expectations and mindset.

Many people come into this industry with very unrealistic expectations and, as a result of those expectations, fail. These people would have likely succeeded if they had come in with more realistic expectations and the right mindset.

When most people hear the word "mindset," they automatically think, "Oh this is going to be a bunch of woo-woo crap that I have no time for." **That's not the case here.** Chapter 2 contains actionable guidelines that are essential in reprogramming your mentality for the road ahead.

The second step to using the book is to understand that there are no guarantees.

This is true in any line of business, but I wanted to make that really clear up front.

To be really successful in Internet Marketing, the following three components are essential: **hard work, quality**, and **time**. If you're willing to put in the hard work, ensure that work is quality, and give your efforts time, Internet Marketing WILL pay out.

If you're looking for an easy solution where you won't have to lift a finger, or if you're willing to do the work but are impatient for results, Internet Marketing isn't for you.

The third step in using this book is to not write it off just because it's affordable.

I've paid up to $8,000 for courses. I've paid $5,000 to attend seminars on the other side of the world. This book and accompanying course that I've built, and plan to continue building, is intended to outperform every course and seminar out there.

Don't get me wrong; I don't know everything. There's so much to know in this industry and there are other marketers teaching things I don't know. However, I can humbly say that ten years of studying my ass off amounts to A TON of knowledge.

So please don't think that just because a course is high-ticket that it *has* to be better than this training. Those courses might be decent, but what I'm sharing is equally high-quality training (and in most instances, **higher** quality training) that's much more accessible to the average aspiring internet entrepreneur. What could be better?

Lastly, use this book to break free.

You *can* build a profitable internet business with this book and accompanying video training alone. That's exactly why I built FIMP! At the end of the day, use this course for what it's intended to do: **to set you free**.

This may sound cheesy or cliché, but when I talk to people in this industry, a consistent theme emerges: **people want to break free of their day job**. Some people want to break free to be able to travel more and want a business that travels with them. Other people want to break free to be able to provide their family with a better life.

Whatever your motivation is, Internet Marketing can help you break free. This is why I've put hundreds of hours into this project.

But I can only do so much. It's now up to you to give it all your effort and learn as much as you can from this training, starting with this book.

1.2 The Only Four Paths to Wealth Online

||||||||||||||||||||||||||||||||||||||||||||||||||||||||||||||||||||||||||||||||||||||||||||||||||||||||||

This section will be breaking down Internet Marketing into four different categories and provide a straightforward, easy-to-understand formula for building a profitable internet business, as well as explaining the core competencies that any aspiring internet entrepreneur needs to be successful.

The Four Paths to Wealth Online: An Overview

Every single online business I've encountered falls into one of four categories:

1. a content-based business monetized through advertising

2. a service-based business

3. an e-commerce business selling physical products

4. a content-based business selling your own digital products

A **content-based business** involves creating a site with loads of valuable and helpful content. Monetization can occur through advertising, which means that you get paid every time someone clicks an advertisement on your site.

A **service-based business** is one where you get paid for completing services for clients. One example is an online writing agency where you charge a certain fee per article. Depending on the difficulty of the topic, and the number of articles required, you can either write the articles yourself or manage a team of writers to write the articles.

Another example of a service-based business is a Search Engine Optimization (SEO) agency where you charge a business owner a monthly fee to get their business website ranked highly in Google search results.

Running an **e-commerce business selling physical products** is another viable path. Physical products may be products that you produce or buy in bulk from a supplier and sell at a markup. E-commerce also provides the option of dropshipping, which eliminates the need to buy in bulk because the customer orders directly from you and the supplier ships the product directly to the customer. You never see or handle the product yourself.

Another possibility is a **content-based business selling digital products** that you create. This is a subset of content-based business, however, instead of selling ad space, you're selling *your* content. Examples of digital products you can create and sell are books, whitepapers, digital courses, audio courses, and even stock photos.

A common misconception about selling a training course, or any digital product, is that it *has* to be about Internet Marketing. **This is incorrect**; there are people making good money selling training courses about other topics.

For example, an Elementary School librarian in the United States created her own curriculums in digital format, which she updates every year and sells for $300 to $400 a pop. Any teacher knows creating curriculum is a time-consuming and tedious process; buying these curriculums at $300 each is a bargain in terms of the hours saved. This librarian now makes about six figures a month selling her digital curriculums to librarians across the United States.

What These Four Paths Have in Common

Every internet business, regardless of which of the four categories it falls under, breaks down into what I call "reverse math."

When setting internet business goals, whichever path you decide to take, remember this simple formula:

 To earn **X** amount of dollars per month, you'll need **Y** customers multiplied by **Z** dollars per customer.

Think of it as an equation for revenue:

<u>Y</u> (customers) x
<u>Z</u> ($ per customer) =
<u>X</u> (goal amount to earn per month)

Let's apply the formula to each of the four paths.

Content-Based Business (Monetized Through Advertising): Reverse Math

One way to monetize a content-based business is through advertising. Let's assume you have a content-based business you're going to monetize through advertising, and that you want to make $10,000 a month. The starting point for most people is Google AdSense, which displays advertisements on a website based on its content (and other factors). One of the ways to make money with Google AdSense is on a "per-click" basis.

If you opt for a per-click program, called Cost Per Click (CPC), you get paid a certain amount for every click that ad on your website gets. Applying the formula:

If you want to make **$10,000 (X)** a month, you'll need **10,000 (Y)** visitors to click the ad on your website if the payout is **$1 per click (Z)**.

The problem with CPC is that most websites are lucky to even get a 3% Click-Through Rate (CTR), which is the percentage of visitors who click on an ad over the total number of visitors to your site.

Given a 3% CTR, if you need **10,000** visitors to click the ad, you'll need roughly **330,000** visitors to your website. The outlook is even more daunting if you have a 1% CTR, which is the common rate for an average website. At 1% CTR, if you need **10,000** visitors to click the ad, you'll need **1 million** visitors to your website a month.

Those are insanely difficult numbers to achieve. Receiving a million visitors a month requires a great deal of content to optimize for search engines and many visitors coming in every single day.

Don't get me wrong, though. There *are* people who earn millions through Google AdSense, so it's not impossible to make a lot of money this way. It's just *really* difficult because most websites will only ever receive tens of thousands of visitors a month, if that. The CPC model is not the best path to monetization for most internet businesses.

Another way to monetize a content-based business is through a Pay Per Lead, or Cost Per Lead (CPL), model. Technically this falls under the umbrella of CPA Marketing, which I'll dig into further momentarily.

With a CPL model, you get paid every time a qualified lead signs up for and expresses interest in a company's products from your website. Companies that employ this model include insurance companies, mortgage companies, and home services. The CPL model generally pays better than CPC.

For example, if you write an article about a specific credit card, and a visitor clicks the link from that article to apply for it, you receive a commission for the lead you just generated for that credit card company.

Yet another way to monetize a content-based business is through other forms of Cost Per Action/Acquisition (CPA) offers, wherein you get paid by what is referred to as the "advertiser" every time a visitor takes a specific action on your site, such as signing up for a newsletter, registering on another website, or signing up for a free trial.

Companies that practice this model include Netflix and FreeCreditReport.com. Here's how it works: when a website owner advertises Netflix's free services and a visitor signs up for that free trial, Netflix pays the website owner a commission. Like the CPL model, the CPA model pays better than the CPC model.

Let's apply the "reverse math" formula to the CPA model, pretending you're getting $10 per free trial:

If you want to make **$10,000 (X)** a month, you'll need **1,000 (Y)** visitors to sign up for a free trial on your website if the payout is **$10 per signup (Z)**.

Given a 1% CTR, if you need **1,000** visitors to click the ad, you'll need roughly **100,000** visitors to your website a month. Getting 100,000 visitors to your site, monthly, is WAY more achievable than getting a million. It's going to take a lot of time and hard work, but it's much more doable than aiming for 1 million visitors each month (using the CPA model).

The reverse math still holds if, instead of advertising, you're monetizing by selling another company's product. Selling a $200 product that gives you a 50% commission means you earn $100 from every sale. Applying the formula:

If you want to make **$10,000 (X)** a month, you'll need **100 (Y)** visitors to buy the product on your website if the payout is **$100 per product sold (Z)**.

Given a **1%** conversion rate (in this case, the percentage of visitors who buy over the total number of visitors), if you need **100** visitors to buy the product, you'll need roughly **10,000** visitors to your website a month. Again, this is a much more feasible number than 1 million, or even 100,000.

Service-Based Business: Reverse Math

One way to monetize a service-based business is to outsource a service. Imagine that you're running a writing service where you outsource the writing to a team in the Philippines and pay $4 per article. In turn, you charge clients $6 per article and profit $2 per article. Applying the formula:

If you want to make **$10,000 (X)** a month, you'll need to sell **5,000 (Y)** articles if you make **$2 per article (Z)**.

Depending on the niche and how good the writers are, it's possible to have 500 customers, ordering 10 articles each, per month.

Another service-based business you can build is a Search Engine Optimization (SEO) agency. This is a specialized industry and is thus considered a high-value business. Getting a company website ranked highly on search result pages is priceless, so, depending on the niche, an SEO agency can charge anywhere from $1,000 to $5,000 a month per client. Applying the formula:

If you want to make **$10,000 (X)** a month, you'll need to get **10 (Y)** clients if you make **$1,000 per client (Z)**.

Acquiring 10 clients may seem easy, but it's not.

It takes considerable experience to get to the point that a client is willing to pay $1,000 for SEO services. If you're willing to put in the hard work, train extensively, and gain experience in a heavy-competition niche, such as real estate, you can eventually make $5,000 per client per month.

E-commerce: Reverse Math

The reverse math formula can also apply to a business selling physical products on its website. Let's say, for example, you're selling a product that makes you a profit of $1 per product sold. Applying the formula:

If you want to make **$10,000 (X)** a month, you'll need to sell **10,000 (Y)** products if you make **$1 per product (Z)**.

However, there's still the conversion rate to consider in this scenario. Given a 1% conversion rate, if you need **10,000** buyers, you'll need **1 million** visitors to your website per month.

If you sell a product that makes a profit of **$10** per product sold, you'll only need to sell **1,000** products to make **$10,000** a month. Given a 1% conversion rate, if you need **1,000** buyers, you'll only need **100,000** visitors to your website per month which, again, is more attainable than 1 million.

Content-Based Business (Selling Your Own Digital Products): A Quick Note

When selling your own digital product, the profit margins are usually at least double than when affiliating with a separate product publisher. The price point for digital products can be quite high, ranging up to thousands of dollars per sale.

However, a big drawback is the time and energy needed to create a digital product, so this typically isn't the first form of monetization to try for. For all you know, you could put weeks or months of time and energy into developing a product that ultimately doesn't sell.

Most people will monetize their site using one of the other three forms of monetization in the beginning and later expand into selling their own digital products to realize two to three times profit margin, and sometimes a multi thousand-dollar value per conversion.

If you're selling someone else's digital product at $100 each, you only need 100 sold to reach your goal. But, if you're selling your own high ticket and high value digital product, you only need to sell two per month to achieve your monthly goals. So, although it's a very "high risk, high reward" path to monetization, and it requires a ton of time and energy compared to the others, it ultimately can be the most lucrative.

Key Takeaways from Doing All That Reverse Math

What does all that mean? What was the point of doing so much math?

By now, the trend should be obvious:

 As your earnings or commissions per visitor go up, the number of visitors you need to achieve your goals goes down.

Reverse math aside, anyone planning to get into Internet Marketing needs to know how to drive traffic. Each of the Internet Marketing paths needs to be combined with traffic to earn massive profit, and that's a lot easier said than done.

This brings me to the topic of **free** or **paid traffic.**

If you happen to have a couple of thousand dollars a month lying around to spend on advertising, that's awesome. Paid traffic can yield results sooner than free traffic. However, if you don't have that kind of budget, don't feel like driving traffic to your site using free tools and resources is impossible. IT'S POSSIBLE, and I'll outline how as we dive further into this book.

The Three Core Competencies You'll Ever Need to Make Money

The four paths to wealth online require two factors to be successful: traffic and one of the following three core competencies.

1. Obtaining the most money for your traffic,

2. obtaining inexpensive high-quality labor, and

3. obtaining inexpensive high-quality products.

Getting the most money for your traffic, also known as Conversion Optimization, is a skill you'll need to develop if you're going down the content-based business path. Whether you plan to run a blog or a YouTube channel, and whether you plan to monetize through advertising or by selling digital products, knowing how to increase the percentage of visitors that click on the ads or buy the digital products on your website will be crucial to your success.

Getting inexpensive high-quality labor is a necessary skill required for a service-based business. Initially, you'll most likely be doing everything yourself. To scale, you'll need to learn how to get exceptional labor at the lowest possible price without compromising quality. The cheaper the labor, the higher the profit margins are, and the more money you're going to make.

Getting inexpensive high-quality products is an important skill you'll need if you want to do business in e-commerce and sell physical products. Whether you're creating the product yourself and having to buy raw materials, or you're having a supplier manufacture them for you, you'll need to learn how to find the best deals on these products and materials. Much like outsourcing quality labor for the lowest possible price, getting high-quality products at a good deal is about lowering your costs to drive profit margins up.

Bringing Reverse Math Full Circle

Internet Marketing can be broken down into the following equation:

ALL four profitable paths to online income =
Traffic + ONE Core Competency.

Internet Marketing is extremely overwhelming. I guarantee if you choose to pursue this track, you're going to get overwhelmed several times along the way. It's perfectly normal to become overwhelmed throughout this process because there is a lot to learn. Acknowledge and understand this early on so that you're aware of when it's happening and know to push through it.

When you start to feel overwhelmed, take a deep breath, review the reverse math again, and remember: *you don't have to learn everything.* Think of the feeling of being overwhelmed as what stands between you and success; what stands in the way of changing your, and your family's, life.

You only have to know ONE core competency inside and out. Combine that with traffic and you'll have a potentially profitable internet business in no time.

Chapter 1 Summary

- How to use this book:
    - Read Chapter 1 and Chapter 2 in their entirety
    - Understand that there are no guarantees
    - Don't write off this book just because it's affordable.
    - Use this course to break free

- The ONLY four paths to wealth online:
    - a content-based business monetized through advertising
    - a service-based business
    - an e-commerce business selling physical products

- a content-based business selling your own digital products

- The reverse math formula that applies to all four paths of Internet Marketing:

  - Y (customers) x Z ($ per customer) = X (goal amount to earn per month)

- The only three core competencies you need to make money:

  - Obtaining the most money for your traffic

  - Obtaining inexpensive high-quality labor

  - Obtaining inexpensive high-quality products

- The formula to Internet Marketing success:

  - All four profitable paths to online income = Traffic + ONE Core competency

 If you prefer to see the training in this book in action, purchase access to the corresponding step-by-step videos it's derived from at: *https://stoppingscams.com/FIMP/*.

Chapter 2: Essential Mindset Training for Success

No one else is talking about mindset, yet it's one of the most important aspects to seeing success in this industry. It's skipped over in almost every Internet Marketing product I've ever seen because the word "mindset" can make some people automatically think of the "if you believe it, you can achieve it" crap. Fair enough.

That's not what this training is.

A small minority of people succeed within Internet Marketing, and a HUGE majority of others fail. Over the years I've learned that the most successful Internet Marketers have qualities that are almost inherent.

These qualities don't have to be hardwired into you in order to be successful. However, you do have to learn them to be able to get through the challenging aspects of this business. The qualities that make some people so much more successful than others are what I'm going to teach in this chapter.

I STRONGLY recommend not skipping any of the lessons in this chapter simply because it's labeled "mindset training."

2.1 The ONLY Way to Guarantee Your Success Online

CHAPTER 2: ESSENTIAL MINDSET TRAINING FOR SUCCESS

The "Get Rich Quick" Myth

I'm going to tell you something that's hard to swallow. Ready? Here's the truth about getting rich quick online:

"Get Rich Quick" is a myth that was created by product publishers.

It just. Doesn't. Exist.

To provide some context, I've personally reviewed hundreds of Internet Marketing products on *StoppingScams.com* and, prior to that, on a site called *NoMoreBSReviews.com*.

Time and time *and time* again, when I encountered products that advertised automated success, shortcuts to income potential, or promises of a "Get Rich Quick" formula of any kind, the product publisher completely failed to deliver on those claims.

I firmly believe, based on these observations, product publishers created the romantic notion that Internet Marketing can be used to "get rich quick" because if they can convince people it's easy, **it's easier for them to sell their product**.

At this point, it's possible some of you may be thinking, "Nope. This guy's full of it. It HAS to be easy. There HAVE to be easy strategies. He just doesn't know them," or perhaps, "I'm going to close this book and follow someone else because THEY can teach me how to get rich quick."

At the risk of seeming like a pessimist, or a "Negative Nancy," I'll simply say this: *I've been in this industry for over a decade*. I know a lot of successful people. I've personally bought and reviewed hundreds of products, which is why I'm confident that any money you spend on a product that claims to teach you how to get rich quick is going to be a waste of money.

Many people think Internet Marketing is synonymous with getting rich quick, taking shortcuts, or something that's easy, but that couldn't be further from the truth.

The Truth About Internet Marketing

Every business takes serious dedication, and Internet Marketing is no different.

You're going to have to learn a lot of new skills and work really hard. If you're willing to put in the time to learn and the effort to build, then **running a profitable internet business is indescribably awesome**. There's really nothing like it.

Even if you're not making money hand over fist, working for yourself AND having complete autonomy in your schedule makes a really big difference in quality of life. Not only can you work from home, you can travel anywhere you want and your business travels with you.

This freedom you get from an Internet Marketing business is what makes the hard work **incredibly rewarding**.

Once you've built your internet business up, put in all the hours, and created a site that generates a ton of traffic, you can get to the point where your business is considered a passive stream of income. It's at that point things will seem easier because your business will continue to be profitable, even when you can only spare five to seven hours a week on it.

But, the time and effort to get to that point is crucial. Even then, there are no guarantees that you'll "get rich quick," or become rich at all.

I feel confident telling you this because of my experience getting to that point. Some of my businesses are currently earning five figures a month in passive income. It took two years of grinding on each one of those projects to get to that point.

With this book and the accompanying FIMP training, you **might** be able to get to the point of passive income within 12 to 18 months. Keep in mind that those months won't be a picnic. Your business needs to be treated like a little baby that requires a lot of nurturing to grow. Eventually that baby is going to make you money, but you have to be willing to put in the work.

The Iron Mindset

I know several Internet Marketers who are doing well for themselves, many of whom are more successful than I am. These marketers include followers from my websites, people I've met at conferences and trainings, and friends from around the world who I've met throughout my Internet Marketing journey.

What I've learned from all of these people who come from different walks of life is that every successful Internet Marketer has one trait in common: an Iron Mindset.

There are three factors to having an Iron Mindset:

1. **Be extremely determined.** Keep in mind that Internet Marketing is the key to your success and changing your life.

2. **Understand this is a non-linear journey.** Typically, in business, earnings go up according to the more a person learns and works. Internet Marketing, unfortunately, isn't like that.

You work, learn, and sometimes get a really good month. The next month could be a completely different story, though. It's important to understand this journey isn't one neat, straight path. You're going to experience peaks and valleys and, over time, reach your goal.

3. **Never give up.** The idea will be tempting, especially when you consider how much work goes into building an Internet Marketing business, how much dedication it takes, and the rollercoaster of experiences you'll face.

   Keep making progress and I guarantee you cannot fail in this industry. If you continue trying, standing up and dusting yourself off after you make mistakes, and continue showing up day after day, *it WILL happen*.

Every Journey Begins with Taking the First Step

The Iron Mindset may seem like an inherent trait for these successful marketers, and perhaps it is. However, there's no reason you can't learn it.

Learning a new mindset won't happen overnight, but you can start forging it today. Begin adjusting and reprogramming your brain starting now.

Remember: this is going to be a long, demanding journey. Expect to get overwhelmed at some point.

Be ready to make mistakes; they're inevitable. Most importantly, keep showing up, keep learning new skills, keep growing and self-developing, and keep creating value in your niche.

I heard a phrase once that stated, "You can measure someone's net worth by how much value they've put into the world." This message really stuck with me because it holds true in most circumstances, so it's a good rule of thumb to live by.

Forging the Iron Mindset now will increase your chances of being successful. It may take six months, two years, or even four years, but *it will happen*.

My Story

Internet Marketing has been the most rewarding experience.

One of the reasons I chose to start an internet business back when I was only 16 years old was because I desired a very specific lifestyle. A lifestyle where I answered to no one but myself.

You won't see me flashing Lamborghinis or shooting a sales video in a Hollywood mansion — that's not how I spend my money.

If that's what your heart desires, **go for it!** Internet business can absolutely make that possible (although the vast majority of people I've seen flash Lambos and mansions in **this** industry are unmistakably trying to take advantage of people; you'd gain more than you'd lose by just setting a "run for the hills" rule when you see it from an online business product publisher).

I got into internet business for the freedom it could provide.

I didn't want the stress of calling in sick. I wanted to be able to take a day off without worrying about consequences. If one of my dogs was ill or dying, I wanted the freedom to be able to take a day off and take care of her. I sought the freedom to take as many days off as I wanted without having to get permission from a boss or supervisor.

In my opinion, being forced to live under someone else's rule is unreasonable. We live ONE life and should be in complete control of it. We shouldn't have our lives dictated by other people.

A couple of other reasons I ventured into Internet Marketing was because I wanted the freedom to travel whenever I wanted and I wanted to be involved in my future children's lives.

These are all the reasons I pushed, shoved, and put everything into building a successful internet business. My wife and I have been able to travel frequently within and outside the US, including South America, Asia, New Zealand, and

Europe, because my business packs up and goes wherever I go.

At this point in my journey, I can afford to work a couple of hours a day and take the rest of the day off because my team members keep everything running.

It's possible, it's achievable, and it's **worth it**.

Internet Marketing changed my life, and it can change yours, too. That's why I'm passing on my knowledge; it's the best gift I can give to the world.

2.2 What to Expect in the Coming Weeks and Months

IIIIIIIIIIIIIIIIIIIIIIIIIIIIIIIIIIIIIIIIIIIIIIIIIIIIIIIIIIIIIIIIIIIIIIIIIIIIIIIIIIIIIIIII

A question I get asked a lot is, "How much time will it take to be successful?" I wish there were an easy answer to this question.

Success isn't going to happen overnight, that's for certain. I can't give a definitive timeframe, either. What I CAN do is provide a general idea of what milestones to expect in the coming weeks and months.

Knowing what milestones to prepare for will make it easier to set realistic goals, even when you're not certain when exactly those milestones will occur.

Realistic goals are extremely important. Setting unrealistic goals makes it more likely that they won't be achieved. The more goals you miss, the more deterred you become, and that makes you more likely to give up. **I don't want that for you.**

The Most Universal Internet Marketing Track

The track described below is one that virtually anyone can do, which means:

- **It has the lowest startup costs.** Starting a business with no budget isn't possible in today's search engine climate. However, unlike a brick and mortar business, you can manage to keep a low startup cost for an Internet Marketing business.

- **It has the fewest moving parts.** Think of a toy robot: the more complicated it is, the more parts it has, and the greater the possibility that one of the parts doesn't line up correctly. After some time, the toy robot is broken, and there's no way to know what went wrong.

  The more moving parts a business has, the more likely it is for something to go awry. In the end, it's difficult to assess exactly what went wrong. What I'm going to teach has the fewest moving parts possible to help maintain a degree of control over the outcome.

- **It's one of the most forgiving.** There are tracks where, even if you do everything exactly right, you can lose thousands of dollars. That's not something you have to worry about with this track.

There are faster and more advanced ways to make money in Internet Marketing. However, they require more investment that is typically spent on advertising, as well as tools to maximize that advertising budget. If you have a lot of money to put into your business, then you'll be able to get results faster.

For now, I want to teach the most cost-efficient and foolproof way to start a profitable internet business.

Time Requirement

Expect to dedicate at least 10 hours of work per week to your business.

GASPS

Let me do you a solid and get some of those initial thoughts out of the way:

"That's way too much time."

"But I have a full-time job!"

"There's so much on my plate right now."

The brutal truth is this:

If you can't give your business at least 10 hours a week, then you don't have any business building a business right now.

I genuinely mean no offense by that. It's my obligation to tell you the truth, and the truth is that if you can only dedicate three to five hours a week to this business, you're VERY unlikely to see success.

If you're serious and actually want to succeed in this industry, it's time to reprioritize a few things in your life and find 10 hours each week to put into your business. If that's not possible, or you'd rather be doing other things with that time, *then just do those other things*. Spend those hours in a way that is going to be more beneficial to you.

For everyone else: how does 10 hours a week sound to you? Does that sound doable? Haven't put down this book yet? Then let's continue.

Most people are concerned with *when* they will begin to see successful results from their efforts. **Plan to see results in AT LEAST six to 12 months**. And by "results," I mean income.

Early signs of success include seeing traffic a bit earlier, organic comments on your blog or videos, or people sharing your content on social media.

Spending more hours on quality work will get you results much faster. For example, if you work 20 hours a week, you're going to see results **twice as fast** as someone who's putting in the bare minimum of 10 hours a week.

The other thing people are concerned with is how much money they're going to be making.

Realistically, aim to see **$800 to $1,000 per month** at the end of 12 months if you work 10 hours per week. Again, working twice as many hours means you can aim a bit higher, such as $1,500 to $2,000 a month.

I hope I'm not making it seem as if 10 hours a week isn't valuable, because dedicating that much time to something is nothing to scoff at. Working at the bare minimum just means it will take a little bit longer to reach your goals. Keep that in mind as you anticipate the road ahead.

"How Much Money Do I Need to Get Started?"

Earlier I stated that it's impossible to start a business with no money in today's search engine climate, so a reasonable question to ask is: how much money will be needed to start?

During the first year you'll need somewhere between **$70 to $110 for startup capital**. This isn't negotiable.

This capital goes mostly towards your website, which is another nonnegotiable. You'll need to buy **a domain name**, which can cost somewhere between $10 to $15 a year, and **quality web hosting** for your site, which can cost between $60 to $96 a year.

If "web hosting" is an alien phrase to you, I dive deeper into this topic in a later chapter. Long story short, web hosting allows you to publish a website on the internet.

A **desktop or laptop computer** is something you'll need to invest in as well. Unfortunately, you can't build an internet business from a tablet or mobile phone. The technology just isn't there yet. It's like trying to build a house with a shoe instead of a hammer.

You may also consider investing in **premium tools** that will make this journey easier. Premium tools aren't necessary because there are free tools available, however, premium tools can save you a lot of time and money at the end of the day. Personally, any chance I get to save time for my business by investing in a premium tool for a reasonable cost, I do it.

If you don't have the means to invest in these essentials, I recommend holding off on pursuing Internet Marketing for now because these are the bare minimum requirements to get started.

Quarter-to-Quarter Milestones

These milestones are a guideline for anyone committing about 15 to 20 hours per week.

Months 1 to 3:
Pushing Through the Trial and Error

During the first quarter, you're going to spend a lot of time rereading this book and your notes, revisiting the training videos, and tinkering with your website and content. Google will become your best friend as you figure out how to do or fix things on your site. The questions will seem never-ending. You may spend hours tweaking one thing that will make you question the decision to get into Internet Marketing.

Be warned: there's going to be a lot of trial and error during this early stage, and it's not going to be easy. The key to push through it is to keep learning, *especially* the technical stuff, because no one is going to hold your hand later on. An independent mentality is extremely important in this industry.

I'm going to do my best to outline every single step of the way, but, at the end of the day, if you encounter any kind of issue, there are millions of users and website owners out there. You can easily do a quick Google search for a solution to most problems.

The good thing about learning everything for the first time is that you'll only have to learn it once. The next time you utilize a new skill, it's going to be a little easier. Beyond that, it will become second nature.

Months 4 to 6:
Second Guessing Everything

In the second quarter, you'll still experience some of the same challenges faced during the first quarter, however, you'll have the skills necessary to overcome them. This quarter, you're going to be less worried about the technical stuff and more worried about overall strategy.

Keep in mind that there's no one to give you feedback and tell you that you're doing everything right. So, during this period it might seem as if you're putting in a lot of hard work and not seeing results.

Too often, I've seen people in the midst of this stage simply quit. The uncertainty of results weighs heavily on them, so they stop producing quality work. These people go from doing careful keyword research and writing 1,500 to 2,000-word posts of high quality, search engine optimized content, to posting five-minute videos. Then, eight months later, they're wondering why they're not seeing results.

The Iron Mindset will play a huge role during this quarter. You've learned all the strategies, technical training, and methods. If after four months it still feels like you're not seeing results, having an Iron Mindset will prepare you to overcome and push through.

Continue producing quality content, even when you're questioning whether you're doing everything correctly. Trust me: *it will pay off.*

Months 7 to 9:
Early Signs of Traction

Depending on your niche and efforts, you're probably not seeing a lot results yet, but you may be seeing early signs of traction, such as traffic to your website and comments on posts.

There are cases of people who landed in a really good niche, worked really hard to put out high-quality content, and, at this point, were already seeing some part-time income. *These are extremely rare cases.* These people are exceptions, not the general rule. The usual trend at this point is seeing some traffic and comments, especially if you're marketing on social media.

Months 10 to 12:
Potentially Generating a Part-Time Income (or More)

If you stuck it out during the most challenging times in the first three quarters, at this point you should start seeing a part-time income. There are people who have begun earning a full-time income by now, but remember: they're the exceptions. Those people are some of the hardest working in the industry, and, frankly, work harder than I do (and I'm a *very* hardworking person).

I wish I could guarantee a full-time income at this stage, especially if you gave Internet Marketing 12 months of hard work, but there simply aren't guarantees in this business. If you followed the training, worked hard, and gave it your best efforts, then you should be earning *at least* a part-time income after 12 months.

High Competition Niches: A Longer Journey

If you're in a high competition niche, add six to eight months to your journey.

When you're in a high competition niche, it takes longer to see results. If you find at month 10 you're still not seeing traffic to your website, it doesn't necessarily mean you're screwed. It just means that it's going to take longer to break through.

High-competition niches include any of the **evergreen** niches. Evergreen niches are full of buying audience members and tend to have high competition as a result. Even though these niches take longer to monetize, once you do, there's no lack of monetization opportunities.

The three biggest evergreen niches are:

1. Health and Wellness (including Health and Beauty)

2. Making Money Online (including Business Opportunities, Forex, and Investing)

3. Relationships and Dating

These niches will always have earning potential if you can get the traffic. However, with a lot more competition, it takes longer to get that traffic.

As you work through each quarter, keep in mind that missing these milestones doesn't necessarily mean you're doing something wrong. As I said before, there are no guarantees in this industry. Push through the difficult moments and continue producing high-quality content. When you're providing value to your audience and the world you're going to reap financial reward.

Setting up Realistic Goals

Aside from expecting to work at least 10 hours per week and planning for this journey to take at least 6 to 12 months, here are a couple of other things to prepare for as you set goals:

1. Above all else, aim for traffic during the early stages.

Qualified traffic is the lifeblood of any internet business. How to get qualified traffic is discussed in detail later on because generating traffic is where a lot of people go wrong in this industry.

The design of your website, how much money it's making, and how you're integrating affiliate offers or advertising should be secondary to traffic in the beginning. Focus on traffic first and everything else will follow.

Once you receive qualified traffic, it can be turned into part-time income, and part-time income can be built into full-time income.

2. Growth will be unpredictable.

Growth can look like an exponential curve: in the first eight months there's nothing, and month nine you earn $200. At month 10 you could earn $1,200, and at month 11 you earn $2,300. It's not always going to look exactly like that, but it's a typical pattern for those who grind.

There will be months when your earnings suddenly drop. This could be due to loss of traffic or search engine rankings going down unexpectedly. Things like this happen and the sooner you're prepared for it, the better you'll handle it.

Make sure to be realistic. You're not going to immediately start earning $5,000 a month. Growth will be gradual, but it's amazing how quickly earnings can snowball once they're initiated.

2.3 How to Guarantee Goals Are Achieved

"When will I make money?"

"How much money can I make?"

These are really common, reasonable questions that are, unfortunately, impossible to answer with any degree of accuracy. I can give you a general idea of what to expect, though.

When You'll Start Making Money

How long it takes to succeed is mainly determined by two factors: competition and effort. A person working 20 hours a week in a really low-competition niche is going to get there a lot faster than a person working 10 hours a week in the same niche.

Aside from competition and effort, there are several other moving parts that can affect how long it's going to take to see income, such as how well you're following what you've learned, the quality of your work, and how well you learn from early mistakes.

How Much Money You Can Make

How much money can be made is determined by how large an audience is, how much of a buying audience they are, and how well the offers in that industry pay.

Having an audience of 100 *million* will provide a much higher income cap than having an audience of 100 *thousand*. That said, having a large audience doesn't mean anything if they aren't a *buying* audience; that is, an audience that is willing to spend money. Furthermore, an industry that pays $100 per offer will provide a much higher income cap than an industry that pays $20 per offer.

This all may seem like no-brainers, but when picking a niche, these factors are often overlooked. Picking the right niche can greatly influence how much income is earned within a certain period of time.

Money-Based Goals: How to Set Yourself Up for Disappointment

Knowing A) that it's impossible to predict how much money one will make and B) how much time is required to see results, **setting money-based goals doesn't make any sense.**

On the surface, it may seem to make sense to set a goal to earn $1,000 a month by the end of 12 months. It's okay to have this kind of goal in mind, but don't get too attached: a lot of the factors that affect this goal are out of your control.

If you set a money-based goal and don't meet it, it's going to feel utterly deflating and defeating. Setting money-based goals are what make people wash out of the industry.

So, what *does* make sense? If you shouldn't be setting money-based goals, what *should* you be basing your goals on?

Task-Based Goals: Setting the Right Kind of Goals

The smartest goals and milestones to set are the ones you're in TOTAL control of. The quality of your content, the word count of your articles, how deep you dive during keyword research, and which key-words you're targeting are all things you control.

You control how many hours you work per week, how efficient you are, how many posts you write in a week, and the quality of those posts. Thus, it makes more sense to set goals like:

"I want to post (X) high-quality articles per week."

"I want to improve my efficiency."

"I need to fine-tune my processes so that for 20 hours of work, instead of posting 1 article, I'm producing two or three articles."

Again, you are in control of the factors required to achieve these goals and how many hours you work each week. Your efficiency and article quality are completely up to you.

Adjusting those factors will make a tremendous difference in your Internet Marketing business. Posting high-quality content regularly, with carefully chosen keywords, will generate traffic. In the right niche, traffic will generate money.

How to Set Yourself Up for Success

Task-oriented goals, rather than money-oriented goals, sets an individual up for success because they're in control of the tasks required to meet the goal. However, this also means missing task-based goals is entirely on the individual.

There's nothing wrong with becoming upset if a task-oriented goal is missed; it's part of the process. You have every right to feel dismayed, but don't wallow in self-pity. Learn from your mistakes and move forward.

If your goal is to earn $1,000 per month at the end of six months, and you don't meet it despite your best efforts, don't be mad at yourself. Remind yourself that money-based goals are out of your control.

An important thing to understand is that no matter how controlled and consistently tasks are executed, the outcome is still unknown. Rest easy knowing you did everything you could and let the chips fall where they may.

At the very least, tweak financial goals so they're less money driven:

"I want to create 100 high-quality posts within the next 12 months and, hopefully, that's going to earn me $1,000 a month."

If at the end of those 12 months you're not hitting that kind of income, then at least you have a really good idea of what works, what doesn't work, and what you should keep doing. Adjust your goals and tasks accordingly.

You're Ready!

I hope you feel much more empowered now than you have ever felt going into this journey. I've been in this industry long enough to know in my heart that starting off with the right mindset is key to success in Internet Marketing. If you drill the concepts in Chapter 2 into your brain and take them to heart, you're set up for success on the journey ahead.

Chapter 2 Summary

||||||||||||||||||||||||||||||||||||||||||||||||||||||||||||||||||||||||||||||||||||||||||||||||

- "Get Rich Quick" is a big myth. Getting rich through Internet Marketing is never quick; it takes hard work and time.

- Success in Internet Marketing is not only measured through financial success; it's measured by how much freedom it allows you to live the life you want.

- The most successful Internet Marketers have an Iron Mindset and never give up.

- You CAN learn to forge the Iron Mindset.

- By working at least 10 hours a week for six to 12 months, you can realistically aim to make

$800 to $1,000 a month at the end of 12 months.

- You need $70 to $110 in startup capital, plus a desktop or laptop computer.

- Months 1 to 3 (Pushing Through the Trial and Error): Lots of learning and trial-and-error, plus learning how to create high-quality content in your niche.

- Months 4 to 6 (Second Guessing Everything): Second-guessing everything you're doing and wondering if you're doing it right.

- Months 7 to 9 (Early Signs of Traction): Seeing early signs of traction, depending on your niche and efforts.

- Months 10 to 12 (Potentially Generating a Part-Time Income): Starting to see enough traffic to generate a part-time income or more.

- High-Competition Niches (A Longer Journey): Add six to eight months to these milestones.

- Aim for traffic above all else during the early stages. Growth can be unpredictable.

- Focusing on task-oriented goals rather than money-oriented goals will set you up much better for success.

If you prefer to see the training in this book in action, purchase access to the corresponding step-by-step videos it's derived from at: *https://stoppingscams.com/FIMP/*.

Chapter 3: Picking and Polishing the Perfect Niche

I've found that most product publishers treat niche selection almost as an afterthought; something to skip through quickly, leaving the majority of their students lost, confused, and wondering what to do next. Niche selection is difficult to teach, and that's why so many "teachers" shy away from digging in deep.

Not me. I'd bet the farm that what follows is the best guidance you'll ever see for picking a niche. Make sure to start this long journey on the right foot by picking a niche that kicks ass.

3.1 Unearthing Your Perfect Niche

When aspiring Internet Marketers consider niches, they're motivated by money and usually select a niche that has the most income potential.

As counterintuitive as it sounds, I strongly encourage against that. Don't select a niche simply because there's good money in it; **select a niche that provides the most value to its audience**, regardless of the potential for money.

Why?

It's likely the niche you've selected is one you have a lot of passion for or experience in. Learning everything about that niche will be much easier if you're writing about a topic you provide a ton of value for. You'll thrive providing the most value, especially when learning the ropes.

A secret to success in Internet Marketing is to focus on providing value to your audience, above all else, and everything else will follow. This applies to whatever track of Internet Marketing you plan to pursue.

More value means more traffic, more traffic means more money, and more money means you can optimize the value you provide to produce even more traffic that turns into even more money. That's when Internet Marketing turns into a full-time living.

When picking a niche, providing value should be at the top of mind; let it direct everything you do from here on out.

Picking the Perfect Niche: What's Best for *You*

Niche selection is a very personal and internal process. **Viable niches come from an internal place**, and that's why it's extremely important to go through the niche selection process.

The only scenario in which someone else would be able to suggest a viable niche on your behalf is if they conducted an extensive interview questionnaire process, reviewed and interpreted your answers, and dug into the niches themselves.

Niche selection is one of the most crucial steps in Internet Marketing because the niche you pick could be the difference between failure and success.

No matter how hard you work or the strategies you devise, if you've picked a bad niche, your business will never amount to anything valuable, regardless of how well everything is executed.

There's a chance you may select a bad niche the first time around, but don't worry - it's not the end of the world. I've had my fair share of bad niches and still manage to run a very profitable internet business.

If you happen to pick a bad niche, dust yourself off and, most importantly, stick with your Internet Marketing business. Remember what it means to you and how it would change your life. The stronger of a hold you have on your "why," the more likely you are to survive challenging moments such as discovering three months in that you've selected a bad niche.

This is precisely why niche selection is being addressed now. The next section details the ins and outs of how to select your perfect niche.

The Dreaded "I Don't Have Any Passions" Niche Struggle

As I've previously stated, niche selection is personal. Thriving in a niche you're passionate about and have experience in is much more likely than if you select a niche you have no background in.

There are three main reasons why a lot of people who start in Internet Marketing struggle to select a niche:

1. They claim to have no passions.

2. They feel as if they have no valuable skills.

3. They feel as if they don't have adequate knowledge about anything.

To find the confidence in yourself to say, "YES, I can *definitely* write about that," you'll need to dig deep and do a little soul searching. The best way to start the niche selection process is by brainstorming a list of previous jobs, experiences, and education.

We'll start broad by addressing questions that will help you list ideas. Then, I'll guide you through refining those ideas so you're left with a handful, or possibly one.

Grab a pen and paper, or open your favorite note-taking application, and let's get started.

Write down everything that comes to mind during this brainstorm. It's important to leave nothing out at this stage.

Brainstorm Part 1: Previous Jobs, Expertise, and Education

The first question we'll address is: **what jobs and/ or expertise have you developed over the years?**

Think about all the jobs you've had in the past, dating back to your very first work experience in high school. Regardless if you went to high school 40 years ago or are currently there, there are definitely pockets of knowledge in these experiences that can be refined into a good niche.

The jobs you've held or expertise you've developed are frequently where you're going to be able to offer the most value. Skills learned as a professional or from a certified program in a particular industry are what give you the expertise, authority, and credibility that are inherently valuable in Internet Marketing. As far as I'm concerned, previous work experience is the best category to pick from.

Also think about the courses you took in college. What training did you receive? What accreditations did you gain? What certifications did you earn? Write all of that down. You'd be surprised at what skills that seemed insignificant at the time could potentially be your key to success.

Don't worry if these are fields or subjects you're not passionate about. A lot of people believe niches should be passion based. Just because you're not passionate about a topic doesn't mean you shouldn't pursue it.

Disinterest in a topic you're knowledgeable in may simply come down to being burned out, however, consider that you offer a lot of value there. Think about how much value you can offer others and how much you're going to help people.

Value vs. Passion: The FIMP Story

A great and tangible example is *First-Time Internet Marketing Profits™*. I've been in the Internet Marketing business for over a decade, so I know that this is an area where I can provide the most value to my audience.

Teaching people isn't necessarily my biggest passion, though. I've actively avoided publishing training to monetize for a long time because I didn't want to be another one of those "Me Too Gurus" who strike it rich once, think they can teach their strategies even though they don't know how to replicate them, yet release an expensive product anyway. They get rich by teaching other people how to get rich rather than teach people how to work through the murk. It took me several years to get to the point where I've experienced enough to bring the best value I could ever bring to my audience.

Even so, teaching is monotonous for me. I don't mean to condescend teachers or trainers, it's just not something I'm personally excited about. I enjoy building new Internet Marketing projects, new Affiliate Marketing sites, eCommerce sites, expanding projects, and expanding my team to accommodate projects that have grown significantly more than teaching.

That said, I'm very passionate about helping people, and if teaching Internet Marketing will help people, then I'm in. I have the opportunity to teach people how to change their lives and empower them with skills to build their own internet business. That's what gets me out of bed every day and moves me to record hours and hours of video and write this book. What excites me is the thought of changing someone's life.

Brainstorm Part 2: Problems You've Faced

At this point, you should have some topics listed from the previous section. So, the second question we'll address is: **what problems have you faced in the past?**

What have you found yourself googling and researching extensively? What things do you consistently find yourself coming back to and doing more research on? Examples of topics include health, dieting, beauty, money, debt, business, investing, relationships, parenting, pets, and many more.

If you want to dig even deeper, ask yourself: **in what areas have you faced problems *and* had a lot of difficulty finding a solution?**

If something comes to mind, then a solution isn't readily available for that topic, which means there may not be much competition in that industry. It'll be easier to establish yourself and position yourself as an authority in that niche.

Examine the topic of debt, for example: if you've been in debt and conquered it, or have struggled with your credit rating and managed to improve it, people will want to know about your story.

Another great example is in the beauty industry: if you've struggled with skin issues, such as acne or Rosacea, or have struggled to find a skincare routine that works with your skin type, people will want to know your solution and how you found it. Although the beauty industry targets mostly women, there's an increasing demand for this type of knowledge for males as well.

If you've faced these types of problems, then you have intimate knowledge of the difficulties, struggles, and emotions involved when dealing with them. In short, **you *are* the target audience**. And if you are the target audience, then you're in the absolute best position to provide value.

The next time you encounter a problem, consider if it would make a decent niche.

Brainstorm Part 3: Hobbies and Interests

The last question we'll address is: **what leisure activities do you enjoy?**

This is where interests and passions play a role. What do you find yourself doing in your spare time? Or, if you *had* the spare time, what would you like to do a lot more of?

Examples of leisure activities include music, photography, sports, and crafts, among others.

Do you play an instrument people want to learn how to play?

Do you enjoy photography, or anything art-related that requires you to create something, such as painting, sketching, sculpture, or woodworking?

Perhaps technology related topics are more of your interest, like coding, 3D printing, or creating mobile applications.

What about sports during your free time? Do you, like me, hold season tickets for your favorite team?

If you choose to focus your niche around an interest or hobby, be prepared to spend more time studying than if you had chosen a niche based on something else. Unless you're already an expert in your hobby, you'll have to develop an intimate knowledge of it so you can build the credibility required to write about that topic.

Something I hear often is: *"I feel like a poser because I don't know how to add value in the industry I'm interested in. I don't feel confident writing about the topic."*

At this point, you should anticipate more legwork when producing content because you need to continuously build knowledge in order to provide value. It's okay if you don't know everything right now as long as you commit to learning as much as possible about your chosen industry.

Keep this running list of ideas tucked away somewhere safe, but accessible, so that when inspiration hits you can add to it. In the future, when you find success with a niche, consider building out another one from your existing list.

3.2 Broad Niches vs. Narrow Niches

This section of Chapter 3 will review the differences between broad and narrow niches: how to know which is which, if you're venturing into either one of the extremes, and when you've hit the "just right" sweet spot.

Broad Niches

NOTE: If you wrote down a broad topic during brainstorming, THAT'S FINE. The point of starting broad is being able to refine.

Dieting, Fitness, and Motivation are broad topics, NOT niches. These topics are entire *industries*. Don't expect to succeed in Internet Marketing if you take on an entire industry.

An important thing to note is the broader you go, the longer it takes to gain traction. The more information you're trying to cover, the longer it's going to take you to get search engine rankings, which means it's going to take longer to get consistent traffic to your website.

How to Narrow Down a Broad Niche

"Men's Fitness" is an example of a subject that's too broad. Writing everything there is to write about men's fitness means writing about different accessories and gear, types of workouts, exercise programs, shoes, supplements, celebrities within the industry, celebrity diets, and a lot more that's related to this single subject.

If you try and cover all of the topics within "Men's Fitness," that's, at minimum, one article per topic. Search engines, especially Google.com, are going have an extremely difficult time recognizing your site as an authority when your articles span so many different topics.

Instead, consider writing about a single topic that falls under "Men's Fitness," such as "Workout Supplements for Men." While it's a specific topic, it falls under the subject of Men's Fitness" and gives you the opportunity to become an authority in that topic. You can write about powders, protein shakes, sleeping aids, the pros and cons of supplements, product comparisons, and product reviews. You can even write about possible health risks, if any.

You'll establish yourself as an authority much sooner by selecting a topic within a subject rather than sticking with a broad subject. The sooner you establish yourself as an authority, the faster your search engine rankings will build. Notice that "Workout Supplements for Men" is narrower than "Men's Fitness," but still broad enough that you can write plenty of content.

Here are a couple of more examples within "Men's Fitness" to give you an idea of how to narrow down a broad subject:

- "Men's Fitness" narrowed down to "Home Fitness Equipment"

- "Men's Fitness" narrowed down to "Kettlebell Exercises"

Let's take a look at a different broad subject: "House Cleaning." A few topics that fall under "House Cleaning" include the best ways to clean a bedroom, bathroom, kitchen, safest cleaning products, the best vacuum cleaners, etc... you get the idea.

"Vacuum Cleaners" is still too broad because it's an entire product category. However, it can be narrowed down to "Robot Vacuum Cleaners" (vacuums that automatically charge themselves and vacuum your house). You can write about different brands of robot vacuums, product reviews and comparisons, discuss their qualities, how well they clean compared to traditional vacuum cleaners, and much more. Now THAT could be a very good niche site.

Another example of a narrowed down niche that stems from "House Cleaning" is "Best Vacuums Under $100." There's a lot to be discussed within this topic, such as traditional versus bag-less vacuums, product reviews and comparisons, warranties, and how easy they are to maintain.

Keyword Identification

Another aspect of niche selection that's seldom talked about, but merits discussing, is what I refer to as "Keyword Identification." What I mean by this is: **will your niche identify itself based on what is searched on Google?**

If you came to me and said, "I've chosen Women's Fitness as my niche," I'd say, "that's way too broad. You need to narrow it down." Your response to that might be, "how about Exercises for Women, or Diets for Women Over 50 Years Old?"

While I can understand that train of thought, the reality is that not a lot of people are searching "Diets for Women Over 50" in search engines.

Kudos for narrowing down a broad niche to a smaller audience, but you won't find *that* particular audience searching for terms like "Diets for Women Over 50" because they're A) more than likely using general terms related to diet and fitness and B) not qualifying themselves by including their age in search terms.

If you can't identify who is and isn't in your audience based on the terms they're using to search the internet for information, you haven't actually narrowed that niche down in a viable way.

So, if you tried to narrow down "Men's Fitness" to "Men's Fitness for Men Over 50 Years Old," you're not going to find a whole lot of search terms. "Older Men" can range anywhere between 40 to 70 years old, so instead of focusing on the age, focus on the problems that audience might encounter:

- "Exercises That Are Easier on Joints"

- "Exercises for Older Men"

- "Exercises You Can Do When You're Injured"

Terms like these open your audience up to people younger than 50 years old who may be injured, have gout, or arthritis.

Broad Niches: Revenue Cap

The broader the niche, the larger the audience, and the larger the revenue cap is going to be. If you only have an audience of about 30,000 people across the world, it's going to be very difficult to get more than a few hundred or thousand dollars a month from that site. If your audience contains a million people, the revenue cap for that site increases.

Instead of earning $700 a month at maximum potential, you have the possibility of making $25,000 a month. There's no way to accurately determine how much more you're going to make, but just know (typically speaking) the broader the content you're covering, the larger the audience, and the more earning potential that site is going to have.

How to Target a Broad Niche the Right Way

Even with everything discussed in the previous sections about refining a broad niche, keep in mind that there's nothing wrong with building a broad authority site. If you absolutely want to, you can do it. You just need to do it the right way: step-by-step and bit-by-bit.

To build a niche site that covers a broad subject, like "Men's Fitness," buy a broad domain that's closely related to that subject. Focus your content first on a topic that falls under the subject's umbrella, such as "Workout Supplements for Men." Over time, aim to dominate the supplement niche with content.

When you've done that, dominate and establish yourself as an authority in another topic, like "Men's Exercise Gear." When you've done *that*, dominate and establish yourself as an authority in another topic, and so on.

When building a broad niche site, tackle topics that fall under the subject's umbrella one at a time instead of trying to dominate all of them at once. That's the best and most successful way to establish a broad authority site.

Going Narrow: When is Narrow *Too* Narrow?

Choosing a niche that's too narrow is just as bad as choosing a niche that's too broad. Sometimes it actually ends up being worse. When a person realizes they have a niche that's too broad, they can start focusing on one topic and ignore all others and still correct their course.

When a person realizes they have a niche that focuses on a single product or topic, there's a big chance they have a domain that specifically ties them to a very narrow topic. This can restrict chances of expanding, and the usual course of action is to dump the site and start over with a new niche.

The reason you can't get too narrow is because you're going to have to write high quality, 1,200 to 1,500-word articles two or three times a week for the next several months (if not years) on this topic. When narrowing the focus from a broad topic, ask yourself, *"how much can I really write about this topic?"*

Let's take selfie sticks as an example. How much can you really write about selfie sticks? Can you see yourself producing two or three articles a week for months or years on a topic like selfie sticks? I don't think so.

How to Know the Niche You Chose is "Just Right"

A general rule of niche selection is: **if you can quickly identify 50 different article ideas for that niche, and dig into each one, then you have a good niche.**

If 50 articles sound too overwhelming, think of it in terms of subtopics: can you think of five sub-topics within that niche that you could dedicate at least 10 articles per topic to?

Or, can you think of 10 subtopics within that niche that you could dedicate at least five articles per topic to? If you've picked a niche well, you can probably do that pretty easily.

What Does Your Brainstorm List Look Like Now?

Review the list you put together at the beginning of this chapter; you should be able to eliminate or refine a lot of those ideas by this point. If you've eliminated them all, that's perfectly fine. Now you know how to *really* think about choosing a niche and when your search is over.

Do this process often enough (and you probably will if you're looking at doing Internet Marketing for the long term) and someday you'll have a refined sense of whether or not an idea is feasible when someone runs a niche past you. You'll be able to quickly determine the strengths and weaknesses of a niche, or it's invalidity.

At the very least at this point you've probably eliminated a handful of your ideas. However, this process goes significantly deeper, so don't get too attached to any of your remaining ideas because you might have to cut them at one of the next few stages of elimination.

Again, that's a good thing. The more ideas you cut at this point, the more likely it is that the idea you end up pursuing is something that's really viable.

3.3 Are You Dealing with a "Buying Audience?"

The concept of a buying audience is simple and not particularly difficult to understand or apply to your business. However, if you don't keep this in mind when selecting your niche, it can be detrimental to your success.

This section of Chapter 3 will discuss what a buying audience is, why it's important, and provide examples of how it works.

What Exactly is a Buying Audience?

Once you've narrowed down a niche, the next question to ask yourself is: **will the people who visit my website and read my articles make a purchase to solve their pain points or answer their questions?**

I can't emphasize enough how important it is to keep this in mind any time you select a niche. Remember when I discussed traffic in the previous chapters, and how it's the lifeblood of your business? Well, traffic will only make you money *when you have a buying audience.*

Beware of Freeloaders

This may come off a little harsh, but freeloaders suck. When dealing with a freeloading audience, the number of visitors to your site will steadily go up, and your income will steadily flat-line.

The unfortunate reality of Internet Marketing is that there are several niches where people almost never make a purchase based on a website's content because they're looking for free information.

A couple of examples of these niches are:

- Song Lyric Websites

- Daily Quote Websites

Both of these sites are niches where the audience is looking to gorge on free information and leave.

Think about it from your own perspective: when you search for song lyrics, are you actually going to buy the music sheet?

The only way to consistently monetize these sites is to add advertisements on them. The problem with doing that is a site that monetizes through ads requires massive traffic for it to be truly profitable. To review this concept, refer back to Chapter 1.

To avoid this trap, create content based on search terms people use when trying to solve a pain point or answer a question that will ultimately result in a purchase.

How to Know If You're Dealing with a Buying Audience

Example #1: Private Problems

You've done it. I've done it. We've all searched for solutions to some very personal problems. When people search for terms such as "Athlete's Foot" or "Ringworm," they're probably looking to solve a problem or ease a pain point, which means they're more likely to make a purchase (possibly more).

The more private the problem, the better. It's not likely people will discuss private problems with friends or family, or post about them on social media. Most people even avoid seeking medical help. People search online long before they do any of those things for private problems.

Example #2: Emotionally Charged Problems

People who are dealing with relationship woes, pets being in pain, or who are facing something complex and difficult will search online for answers. These people are also likely to make purchases to solve their problems.

Example #3: Product Related Searches

People searching for terms related to a product are probably going to make a purchase or do research first before making a purchase.

The terms people use to search for information evolve the closer they are to buying. Initially, they may use the term "Best ___," ("Best Vacuums" or "Best Protein Shake") and use the term "___ versus ___" ("Bagless versus Bagged Vacuum Cleaners") further along their research for head to head comparisons. A bit further along the buying stage, people may start using the term "[Brand] [Model Number] Reviews" to see reviews for a specific model.

Try to aim for high-priced products. People looking to buy a high-priced product tend to research a lot before they actually purchase the item. The more helpful your content is, the greater the chance they'll buy through you.

Don't Just Aim for The Final Solution

Getting a buyer in your audience to the last step of the buying process doesn't mean you only have to write about the final solution. There are plenty of opportunities in between where they are and the final solution where you could produce content to monetize. Don't ignore these opportunities because you're focused on the final solution.

For example, if someone is looking to renovate a house, a way to monetize your site is by selling contractor services. However, there are other ways to monetize your site, such as writing about tools and ingenious renovation hacks. You may be able to walk your audience through a do-it-yourself solution that would mitigate and completely solve their problem.

Guides are also a great way to monetize a site. Continuing with the example of home renovation, you could write a guide to different types of kitchen cabinets or the best kitchen appliances.

There is a lot of content to create along the way that will entice your audience to make a purchase decision.

I encourage you to create as much content as possible around your niche to establish yourself as an authority. The more articles you publish, the higher your chances are of getting high rankings.

Review-Based Websites: Who Should Pursue Them?

Review-based sites can be considerably profitable because the individual searching for reviews is typically in the late stages of the research process and more likely to purchase.

However, unless you can buy the products yourself and experience them first-hand, it's going to be difficult to find a way to add more value than your competition when you only produce articles from second-hand information.

If you can afford to buy the products, or if you can come up with a clever way to get your hands on them without purchasing them, you'll have a huge advantage. This is especially true in the technology industry where there's a high barrier of entry. Not a lot of people can afford these gadgets, and if you can provide first-hand insight into using these gadgets, then that's worth something to your audience.

Remember that success depends greatly on how much value is offered. If you can't get products and provide a thorough review from using them rather than obtaining the information elsewhere, it's going to be difficult to add value.

Getting into a High-Priced Product Niche When You Can't Afford It

High-priced product niches are often lucrative, and review-based sites are great for monetizing them. But what can you do if you can't afford to buy the products?

One path into a high-priced product niche is to identify the pain points and questions surrounding a product. Call your audience's attention to the most important things as they're going through the buying process by answering questions like, "What features should one be looking for? What features are nice to have, but not necessary? How do you know if a product is counterfeit?"

Instead of doing side-by-side cellphone reviews, discuss the features within certain cellphones and what to look out for. Write an article about phone usability in general: what makes a phone usable, which cellphones are the easiest to use, etc.

Here's another example: instead of doing reviews or comparisons of computers, explain things like

RAM, processors, the difference between AMD and Intel Processors, which one is superior to the other, different types of monitors, and so on.

People in the market for computers search for this information and find it on multiple websites instead of going to a single resource that has it all. Position yourself as a credible authority and earn money through affiliate links without having to buy computers to review.

3.4 Competition: Why It's Actually a Good Thing

Competition is something that aspiring Internet Marketers get anxious about, however, a little competition is actually a good thing. If a lot of Internet Marketers are competing in a niche, it's a sign there's money to be made there. More importantly, *money is already being made.*

The more competition there is in an industry, the more examples you can find, and the better idea you have of what works and what doesn't work.

The easier competing sites are found, the easier it is to study and discover how to stand out and provide more value than them. The sooner you figure that out, the sooner you can be in their ranks or even outperform them.

How to Beat the Competition

Find a way to provide more value than your current competitors in your niche and it's only a matter of time before you topple them. As long as you continue publishing high-quality content, you WILL break through.

The most important thing to remember about competition is that you don't necessarily have to compete toe-to-toe with your competitors. If you can't provide more value, provide the same value through a different medium. For example, if your competitors publish written content, be the one who publishes videos.

The One Exception

In general, competition is good news, but there is an exception. If everything in your niche is dominated by the same three to five famous and established heavy-hitters, and you're seeing these same few competitors on the first page of search results over and over again, it's probably more beneficial to pursue a different niche.

A good example of this is the company Amazon. Amazon appears two to three times on the first page for a lot of product search terms. If that's the case for you, then it's probably wise to find a different niche.

Another great example is the health niche. If you're finding authoritative health sites, such as *Health.com* or *WebMD.com*, that have a strong hold on the niche, it's probably time to find a different one.

The Most Competitive (And Most Profitable) Industries

The following industries are often referred to as evergreen niches because they have always been the most profitable industries for people running Internet Marketing businesses regardless if it's a blog, an Affiliate Marketing site, or eCommerce site. These niches also tend to be the most competitive *because* they're the most profitable:

- Health, Wellness, and Beauty

- Make Money, Investing, and Business Opportunities

- Relationships and Dating

If you can get traffic from these industries, chances are you're going to make a pretty decent amount of income. However, chances are there's going to be higher competition.

The *NoMoreBSReviews.com* and *StoppingScams.com* Story

When I entered the Internet Marketing product review space, almost all the content I could find about each product was positive. No matter which search terms I used on Google or YouTube, all I found were positive recommendations. I quickly learned that this was the norm because it's how people monetize their sites: with positive reviews.

They weren't giving honest reviews, though. Most "reviewers" weren't even *buying* the products. They were simply claiming:

"This product is great! Buy through my affiliate link."

"It's awesome and fulfills everything it said it would, and more! Buy through my affiliate link."

I became fed up with these reviews because **the majority of recommended products were absolute crap**. How did I know this? Because I'd purchased a lot of them over the years as a result of glowing recommendations from other bloggers.

Ultimately, I decided to enter the Internet Marketing space to provide honest product reviews. The traditional school-of-thought is that if you go into a niche and review products negatively, then you can't make any money. Who's going to buy products that you've reviewed negatively?

However, as I was going through these products and writing honest reviews, I found products that were actually really good. They were fulfilling their sales claims and were of much higher quality than the other products I was reviewing. Through reviewing *all* the products honestly, people came to believe what I said about them, negative or positive. Over time, people found their way to high-quality and legitimate products through my affiliate links.

I could have been more strong-handed in how I funneled people into those products by leveraging the bad products. It would have been as easy as stating:

"This is a bad product. This is a good product, though. Go buy this one!"

I never ventured down this path because I felt that tactic was ethically questionable. My number one priority was, and will always be, helping people. I wanted to keep that at the core of my business. If you help people they will stick with you, follow your training, dig through your site more, and ultimately make you money.

 I started *NoMoreBSReviews.com* by producing honest reviews about Internet Marketing products. Eventually, I built *StoppingScams.com* to be a more holistic site that goes beyond reviews and incorporates training and knowledge to prevent people from getting scammed.

The best way to prevent people from getting scammed is to provide high-quality training so they don't have to purchase any more products. At the very least, when people evaluate products, they have a much better understanding and realistic perspective.

And that's ultimately why I created FIMP and published this book — **to give you ALL of the education you need to protect yourself from getting scammed.**

3.5 (Painless) Internet Marketing Economics

I hope your eyes didn't glaze over when you read the word "economics." This is a subject I really wish someone had called to my attention when I was picking a niche, so I wanted to spend a little time discussing a few simple Internet Marketing economics that are important to understand as you move forward.

Commissions

The cheaper the products in your industry are, the more you have to sell to achieve a certain monthly income. This can be a problem because it means you need more traffic. The more traffic you need, the less likely that income is achieved.

On the other hand, the higher the commission, the fewer products you have to sell. For example, if you're selling a product worth $300, and receive a 5% commission from each sell, you'll earn $15 per product sold.

On the contrary, if you're selling a $10 product, and receive a 5% commission from each sell, you'll earn $0.50 per product sold. You'll need to make fewer $15 commissions to hit your target income than the $0.50 commissions. Thus, you're much more likely to succeed and make a decent income off a lower amount of traffic selling a $300 product than a $10 product.

Commission Percentages

Another factor to consider is a commission's percentage. For example, a $30 product that gives you a 70% commission ($21) will pay more than a $300 product that gives you a 5% commission ($15). For the same volume of traffic, you'll sell more of the lower-priced product than the higher-priced one because of the lower barrier to entry. This is usually the case for digital products.

Don't try to sell a high number of low-percentage, cheap products. Instead, try for digital products that have higher percentage commissions. Sell physical products that cost $50 or more and give lower percentage commissions.

Free Trials

Another monetization opportunity to consider is going into industries that offer free trials you can refer people to. It costs visitors nothing and you get paid per person who signs up and submits their lead information through your affiliate link. There are actually many different industries that use free trials, such as movie streaming services, credit repair, insurance, mortgage, and even supplements.

3.6 Good Niche or Bad Niche?

The best way to teach complex concepts is to give some concrete examples, especially when teaching beginners, so I'm going to dissect a few niche examples and explain why they're good or bad.

Women's Clothing: Bad Niche

"Women's Clothing," unfortunately, is too broad to be a good niche. Besides that, the vast majority of products you can sell are less than $50 with a low-percentage commission. You're not going to find a lot of high-percentage commission products in the women's clothing niche.

Alternatives to "Women's Clothing"

A better and more specific niche in this industry is "Women's Exercise Clothing." There's a lot of information to write about and, more importantly, a lot of women's exercise apparel is very expensive and could exceed the $50 threshold I mentioned. Even though commissions would be on the lower end, they'd be workable.

Another example of a viable niche is "Affordable Fashion Tips." Topics could include "how to shop at thrift stores," "how to find really good deals online," "when is the best time to shop," and any other terms that would make you an expert deal-hunter for women's clothing.

Products in this niche will still likely be less than $50, however, you could persuade visitors to buy an entire outfit and get commissioned on each item (top, bottom, accessories, and shoes) by including sections on your website that target "Women's Outfits Below $100." It's easier to persuade women to buy an entire outfit if you produce high-quality content that explains how to piece together fashionable outfits for the lowest cost possible in conjunction with tips on how to find the best deals.

Dachshund Discectomies: Good Niche

For those who aren't familiar with dachshunds, they're a breed of dog that are commonly compared to sausages because of their long body and short legs. A discectomy is a surgical procedure to remove one or more vertebral discs.

This is a good niche because it's specific enough to allow for ranking high in search engine results, but it's also broad enough of a topic that you could create a lot of high-quality content for it.

I'm personally familiar with this topic. About three years ago, one of my dachshunds blew a disc in her back and she needed to undergo a discectomy. It was a very difficult time, both emotionally and financially. This is the perfect example of a real-life experience that makes you think, *"this would be a really good niche"* because you're dealing with an emotionally-charged problem for a passionate audience.

I'm certain all you animal lovers out there can relate to the feeling of uncertainty and helplessness that would have been eased if you'd had more resources available during a difficult time with a pet. Now, because you're familiar with the procedure or treatment plan, you can provide support and resources for those who are going through the same thing.

Contrary to what your instinct may be, there's actually quite a lot to write about in this niche: Intervertebral Disc Disease (IVDD) and what it is, the details and cost of a discectomy, how to finance the operation so it's affordable, what recovery involves, how to modify your home to make it easier for your pet to move around post-operation, and much more.

The monetization opportunities are there, too. You could outline the details of pet insurance, the different companies who offer it, and who should opt for it and earn commissions for every pet owner who submits their information for a free quote. There's even an opportunity to sell products that help pets post-surgery. If you get enough traffic, you could launch a Kickstarter campaign to manufacture physical products you sell yourself. Finally, you could publish a book that walks pet owners through the path to recovery.

Best Phone Cases: Bad Niche

I did say the term "Best ___" tends to be good to write about, but phone cases are an exception because they're a low-cost product with low percentage commissions. There are top-quality phone cases that cost up to a few hundred dollars, but they're few and far between. Another pitfall of phone cases is that there isn't a lot of content you can create about them because the technical specs to compare products with are limited. You'll want to gouge your eyes out after a few weeks of trying to find unique angles to write about phone cases.

Alternatives to "Best Phone Cases"

To make this niche workable, broaden your topic and create a more holistic website that incorporates phone protection, phone insurance, phone replacement, and phone repairs. Tackle each topic as an individual niche site or one-by-one as parts of a single niche site.

Your content could focus on the best protective phone cases for impact or water and allow you to carve out a niche where phone cases are going to be above $50 because they're specialized cases for very specific pain points. Similarly, another topic to focus your content on is phone insurance and compare carrier insurance coverage to coverage from third parties. The commissions here could be handsome depending on the company.

You could discuss the best options for repairing phone screens, what to do immediately after dropping your phone in water, and how to safeguard your phone against water damage. A lot of people can relate to these pain points, so your content is more likely to be shared.

3.6 GOOD NICHE OR BAD NICHE?

Eventually, you could aim for broader content, like phone protection and replacement options, and use the blog as a pushing off point for launching your own phone cases with a crowdfunding campaign.

Drone Reviews: Good Niche

For those who aren't familiar with drones, they're miniature unmanned helicopters that carry cameras and are used in a wide range of activities, such as surveying land for real estate purposes, search and rescue, and wedding videography.

A drone review website is generally a good niche, but it's a bit challenging to add value because the products can be costly. If you can't afford to purchase all the drones on the market to review, you'll need to come up with a unique angle to break into this saturated niche where first-hand experience is unnecessary to provide value to your audience.

A buying guide that outlines what components to look for, what components are best, and what the different metrics and specs mean when comparing drones side-by-side is a great way to monetize a drone site. A drone gift guide to help people purchase the absolute best drones for a friend or loved one is another profitable option.

Many drones on the market cost up to several hundred dollars each. Even if your commission percentage were 3% to 5%, that could be $20 to $40 for each one you sell. So, although a bit challenging, drone reviews are a good niche.

Tattoo Removal: Good Niche

You probably wouldn't know it if you haven't gone through tattoo removal yourself, or if you haven't at least thought about having a tattoo removed, but there's A LOT of information out there regarding the tattoo removal process. The different types of lasers, different aspects of recovery, and pain management are only the beginning.

When getting a tattoo removed, your skin is being burned by lasers. As with burns in general, the skin needs to be treated carefully. So, one of the topics to focus your content on is the best creams to use on newly treated tattoos.

Surprisingly, there isn't a lot of competition in the tattoo removal space. It's really easy to add immense value because, as I've mentioned, there are several topics to write about. In addition, regrettable tattoos are a big motivating factor for this particular audience. How many people have tattoos that are connected to a relationship gone wrong or are preventing them from landing a decent job?

The biggest challenge with this niche is not going to be having too little material to write about, how to add value, or how to overcome the competition. The biggest challenge for this particular niche is going to be how to monetize it. Tattoo removals are pricey; my personal tattoo removal sessions are about $300 *each*, and that's not even the most expensive option. Many people consider tattoo removal but opt against it because of the cost. However, if the traffic exists, an option to consider is a book that addresses all the need-to-know about tattoo removal. Depending on the content, you can price the book anywhere between $10 to $20.

Seeing even more traffic? Monetize your site by selling leads to tattoo removal clinics. This route may seem intimidating, but it's actually very doable. If you identify at least one clinic in every major U.S. city, you could hire a programmer to write a script on your website that changes what clinic a person is referred to based on their location. Then, you could set up a phone number that tracks the leads you send to clinics so they'll know those leads are from you. You could eventually expand this service to every major city around the world. These are high-value leads that could be worth $5 to $20 each. The clinic I go to makes several hundred to several thousand dollars from every patient.

The lead route can be intimidating and requires learning about the process if you haven't sold or tracked leads before. However, if it's the difference between your site generating $1,000 a month or $15,000 a month, you'll make it happen.

Good or Bad Niche: Key Takeaways

A buying audience isn't enough; you need to be careful not to go too narrow or too broad. In addition, receiving hundreds of thousands, or even millions, of visitors a month isn't likely, so set realistic expectations like 500 visitors a day. With this in mind, remember that you need large enough commissions that make sense.

Review-based sites are good, but if you can't afford to buy all the products for reviews, **make sure you can write a lot of content surrounding the topic.** Add value by producing high-quality content.

If you have a buying audience and a great deal of topics to write about, **there will be a way to monetize, even if you have to create it**. A buying audience in a niche that isn't too broad or too narrow plus a niche you add value to equals monetization opportunities. You may just have to get a little inventive and create them yourself.

3.7 When to Move On: Making Sense of the Tornado Inside Your Head

In this section of Chapter 3, I'm going to recap and connect all of the topics discussed in this chapter. Keep in mind that even if you're still a little bit confused and overwhelmed, you know so much more now than you did when you started. Even though it may not feel that way, you are set up for success better than at least 90%, if not 99%, of people that go into this industry.

Things to Remember

Niche discovery takes time. This may be difficult and overwhelming, but deciding on a niche takes time. It's crucial enough to the success of your business that you actually *want* to take the time to really think about it because it's going to determine whether you succeed or fail in the long run.

Even the worst-case scenario is not that bad. There's a point where you just have to jump in. Even if you end up picking a bad niche, you're going to learn from the experience and move toward success. You'll get the knowledge and experience that is invaluable when you find the niche you end up making a living in.

Give it a shot! Plenty of people have succeeded in this industry before you without remotely this much guidance. Many of them just picked a niche, rolled with the punches, and made it work. So, at this point, even if you don't feel totally confident in your choice, just give it a shot!

Recap: The Core Concepts of Picking a Niche

The best niche is one where you provide the most value. Providing more value means you're more likely to profit from that niche and succeed.

Don't pick an entire industry as your niche, and don't paint yourself into a corner by going too narrow. Don't take on niches that generate thousands of visitors daily, and don't run out of content to write.

Choose a niche with a buying audience. Make sure your audience is willing to make purchases to solve their pain points or answer their questions.

Competition is your friend! It's not something to be scared of but a sign of your niche's profitability.

Choose a niche either with digital products that have high commission percentages or with physical products that are high value (>$50). The higher your commissions, the fewer conversions you need, and the less traffic you need, the more likely you are to succeed.

There are plenty of monetization opportunities if you let your creative juices flow. Giving away free trials, generating leads, and creating your own books and courses are all legitimate ways to make money.

As with all rules, there are exceptions for each of these points, but these are good general guidelines.

When to Let That Niche Go

Two justifiable reasons for letting a niche go are:

1. Feeling burned out and
2. feeling boxed in.

People select niches they've worked in for years because, as mentioned earlier in this chapter, the topic you have the most expertise in is where you can offer the most value. However, some-times even the best motivation to help others won't be enough.

People burn out, especially those who have been forced to live and breathe a niche for too long;

they simply can't work in it anymore. Other times, the content well runs dry and people run out of things to discuss. You'd feel trapped and boxed in, too. When you reach this point, it's over. There's no coming back from those feelings.

If you find yourself in either situation, don't beat yourself up. Most Internet Marketers, even the successful ones, didn't get their niche right the first time.

Fail early, fail fast, fail often. The more you fail, the more you learn. Our successes are made of the failures we've had along the way. We refine, we improve, and we get better. As long as you keep at it, you're going to be successful.

Progress is the goal, not perfection. You may not have the perfect niche, but it's better to launch into something now and spend months making it profitable than spending those months tossing and turning, trying to find the perfect niche.

When Is It Time to Press Forward?

Don't linger on thinking about your niche for more than 24 to 48 hours. Any longer than that, and it's very easy to get paralyzed and stuck in the selection phase. Review everything you've learned about niche selection and then make a decision.

Momentum is one of the most crucial things to becoming a successful Internet Marketer and owning a profitable internet business. The longer you end up stuck in one place, the longer it takes you to succeed, and the more likely you are to quit.

Even if everything doesn't turn out perfectly, you're learning, you're becoming better, and you're taking strides towards success. Even if you are making mistakes, you are making progress whether you realize it or not.

Revisiting the Brainstorm List

Do you still have your brainstorming list? You have two options: either choose the best option from the list or go through the niche selection process again with the knowledge gained from Chapter 3. You'll probably come up with fewer ideas now that you know more, but they'll be much better.

If you're *still* stuck, Google it. No kidding. Lots of people are talking about different niche ideas online. Go through some of them using everything you've learned in this chapter and see if there's anything worth pursuing.

Whatever path you go down, use your best judgment and make a decision within 24 to 48 hours of beginning the selection process. Don't get sucked into a black hole. Make a choice, commit to it, and, at the end of the day, keep reminding yourself that the worst-case scenario is not that bad.

Wrapping It Up

Niche selection is an essential skill to master if you want long-term success in this industry with multiple streams of income. Everything discussed in this chapter and the in-depth knowledge you've gained should empower you to decide on a niche at this point.

Chapter 3 Summary

||||||||||||||||||||||||||||||||||||||||||||||||||||||||||||||||||||||||||||||||||||||||||||||

- Don't go into a niche just because there's good money in it; go into a niche where you can provide the most value.

- There's always a chance that you'll pick a bad niche the first time, but that's not the end of your Internet Marketing journey. Pick a new and better niche and press forward.

- The first three questions to ask yourself when brainstorming are:

  o What problems have you faced in the past?

○ What jobs and/or expertise have you developed?

○ What leisure activities do you enjoy?

- The broader your niche is, the longer it will take to get traction, and selecting too-narrow niches are just as bad as choosing too-broad niches.

- As you narrow down your niche, also ask yourself: Will your audience identify themselves by what they search on Google?

- The broader the content you're covering, the larger the audience, and the more earning potential that site is going to have. If you absolutely want to establish a broad authority site, the right way to do it is one niche at a time.

- How to know if your niche size is just right: Come up with at least five subtopics that you can write 10 articles about each, or 10 subtopics that you can write five articles about each.

- The more ideas you eliminate at the start of the niche selection process, the more likely it is that the idea you end up pursuing is something that's really viable.

- A buying audience is an audience that will likely make a purchase to solve their pain points or answer their questions.

- Traffic without a buying audience is unlikely to translate into an income. You need to create content that is based on search terms that people use when trying to solve a pain point or answer a question that will ultimately result in a purchase.

- Good examples of buying audiences include those who are searching for information about private problems, emotionally-charged problems, and product specifications.

- High-priced product niches are good for monetization as this type of niche provides a lot of opportunities for monetization along the buying process.

- Competition is not something to be afraid of; it's a good sign that your chosen niche is profitable. The exception to this general rule is when the same few heavy-hitters in your niche dominate every search term you look up; then you're probably in the wrong niche.

- To survive and stand out in a competitive niche, you need to add more value, add value in a unique way, or add value through a different medium.

- The most competitive (and most profitable) industries are:

CHAPTER 3 SUMMARY

- o Health/Wellness/Beauty

- o Make Money/Investing/Business Opportunities

- o Relationships/Dating

- The cheaper the products in your industry, the more you have to sell. That means you need more traffic and the more traffic you need, the less likely that it is to happen. Conversely, the higher the commission, the fewer you have to sell.

- Having to get fewer conversions sets you up for success so much better than needing a ton of conversions.

- Don't try to sell a high number of low-percentage, cheap products; instead, try to sell digital products that have higher percentage commissions, or sell physical products that are $50 or more that have lower percentage commissions.

- A buying audience, in a niche that isn't too broad or too narrow, and a niche that you can add value to, equals monetization opportunities.

- It's better to launch into something right now and spend months making it profitable than spending those months tossing and turning trying to find the perfect niche.

- The two most justifiable reasons for getting out of a niche are feeling burned out or boxed in.

 If you prefer to see the training in this book in action, purchase access to the corresponding step-by-step videos it's derived from at: https://stoppingscams.com/FIMP/.

CHAPTER 3 SUMMARY

Chapter 4: The Foundation (Building Your Website)

Aspiring Internet Marketers ask me all the time, "Do I have to build a website?" The answer is indisputably yes. The problem is that building a website is hard, particularly the first time. In fact, this is often viewed as one of the biggest challenges in building an internet business.

I have good news for you, though: building a website doesn't have to be hard or complicated. Follow this chapter, step-by-step, and you'll have a website up and running in no time.

4.1 "Winter Is Coming:" Preparing Your Website Setup and Design

The HBO series *Game of Thrones* is frequently quoted for Ned Stark's famous line, "winter is coming," which means to prepare for difficult times.

Website building is indeed difficult, and if you're not a website designer or developer by trade, you're in for a difficult time. However, I'm about to equip you with everything you need, from setting expectations to actual rundowns, to every tool you'll need.

The creation of a website is the tangible starting point for your internet business because as soon as your website is built, it all becomes very real. It can be a bewildering and confusing time, so I'm determined to help you temper a mindset that sets you up for success.

Establishing Your Mindset

The best mindset to have going into this stage, particularly if it's your first time, is knowing that regardless how challenging things are, or how angry and frustrated you become, at the end of the day, what you're doing is 100% necessary. There's absolutely no way to build a stable, profitable internet business without a website.

Trying to run an internet business without a website is like trying to run a brick and mortar store selling things out of the trunk of your car. Everything works better, is simplified, and under control if you're operating an online business from your own website.

The Good News

Website building is simply a technical step that's standing between you and the successful Internet

Marketing business of your dreams and a better future. The sooner you tackle a website, the closer you are to achieving your goals.

The good news is that you only have to learn how to build a website once. You'll encounter roadblocks that you'll need to research and overcome on your own. Once you learn how to handle them, though, you'll know exactly what to do the next time those roadblocks pop up. Over time, you'll see the amount of time spent researching go way down and your productivity go way up.

"Wasted Time" is Not Actually Wasted

There will be times when you'll encounter an issue that will take hours to troubleshoot. HOURS. By the end of it, when you finally figure out the solution, you'll feel like those hours were wasted. Rest assured, they weren't. During those hours you gained knowledge that prepared you for a similar problem down the road and you'll be better equipped to handle it.

Progress is Slow

Between all the research and awkward navigating, it'll sometimes take hours to complete a simple task. It's important to remember that the first time you build a website will be slow-going. In time, however, the process will become easier and second nature to you.

The Default Mode: "I'm On My Own"

In general, a self-seeking, independent mentality is necessary to successfully create a website and online business. There are millions of website owners who aren't developers who are using the same tools and are going through the same challenges as you. Just like everyone else who's starting out, you need to learn how to figure everything out on your own. There are plenty of resources at your fingertips; look for the answer first before seeking help.

It's a matter of having the default mindset of "research first, ask questions later" that will get you through this process. The only person you can truly depend on is yourself. You can't rely on someone holding your hand through the entire process of building a website.

What I'm going to outline in this chapter is the general process of building a website. If you get stuck on a problem that I skip over or don't discuss, feel free to research it. Researching on your own is a skill you need to develop early, even when you're being guided.

4.2 The Anatomy of a Perfect Domain Name

IIIIIIIIIIIIIIIIIIIIIIIIIIIIIIIIIIIIIIIIIIIIIIIIIIIIIIIIIIIIIIIIIIIIIIIIIIIIIIIIIIIIIIIIIIII

The two essential components of building a website from scratch are:

1. the domain name and
2. hosting.

In the next two sections of Chapter 4 I'm going to discuss domain names: how to choose one and how to acquire one. Choosing a domain name is more time-consuming than people think, but it can be broken down into a simple set of rules.

Things to Know Before Choosing a Domain Name

People become alarmed when they can't find and choose a domain name within an hour. That's perfectly normal. It usually takes one to four hours to pinpoint a domain name, but it can also take six to eight hours over the course of two or three days.

Choosing a domain name is not something that's possible to do within 10 minutes because there are checkboxes you want to make sure and check to ensure the domain's workability. It's going to take time to find a really good domain name, especially in somewhat saturated niches, but we're going to look at tools that will help you immensely.

Changing Domain Names

Can you change your domain name if it's wrong? The short answer is **NO**. The long answer is a little more complicated than that.

There is a way around selecting the wrong domain name, but it requires building a different website on a different domain name and transferring the content of the old site to the new one. It's a very technical process that's time-consuming and not something you want to spend your valuable time doing. So, you definitely want to get the domain name right the first time.

Beware of "Analysis Paralysis"

Falling into what I call "analysis paralysis" is easy to do because there are a lot of factors to consider when selecting the ideal domain name. It's important to remember that you're not going to find the "perfect" domain. Do the best you can by following this guide and using the free tools I'm going to share and hopefully you'll get something, not perfect, but really, really good.

What Makes a Good Domain Name?

Old-school training dictates that an Exact Match Domain, or EMD, is the ideal domain name. EMDs are domain names that precisely match the search term that will drive traffic to your website. In the Men's Supplements niche, people are using the term "men's supplements" in search engines, so a domain name that matches that exact phrase, like *MensSupplements.com* for example, would constitute as an EMD. According to the old-school practice, websites with an EMD shoot straight to the top of search engine results pages.

It didn't take long for spammers to abuse this advantage by purchasing EMDs, building sites with low-quality content, and watching their rankings zoom to the top without the hard work of building an actual helpful website. After a while, Google caught on and penalized EMD sites with low-quality content.

At the time people who owned a legitimate EMD site with high-quality content, useful internal and external links, and great site structure weren't penalized for having an EMD site.

If you've gone through training that heavily promotes EMDs, forget it; EMDs aren't going to give you an advantage over the competition anymore. So, what does?

Valuable content.

This early in the game it doesn't matter what keywords are or aren't in your domain name. The site will get ranked as long as you have valuable content.

The Anatomy of a Perfect Domain Name

What makes a domain name as close to perfect as you can get? Here are some basic rules listed in order of priority:

1. Use a ".com" domain suffix.

You'll have a greater chance of ranking high in search engine results and getting brand recall with a ".com" suffix than any other domain suffix.

Think about it from your audience's perspective: if a person goes to your website once, manages to catch the brand name, and wants to go back to your site at a later date, they're going to type your domain name followed by ".com." It's second nature for most people, including you and me.

People will struggle to find your website if it's registered under any other domain suffix. They may eventually find your site through Google searches, but that can turn into a multistep endeavor that's easy to ditch.

2. Make your domain name memorable, brandable, and easy to spell.

The easier a domain name is to remember, the easier it is for it to be shared with others in person or through social media.

3. Shorter names are best.

Try to limit your domain name to two or three words so people can recall it easily. Admittedly, this particular rule might conflict with Rules 1 and 2 and make deciding on a domain name challenging. If you get really stuck trying to make sure your domain name follows all the rules, prioritize a ".com" suffix and making it memorable rather than shorter.

4. Avoid hyphens and numbers.

Hyphens and numbers are *technically* allowed in domain names, but this rule exists for a practical reason: hyphens are associated with low quality websites, and numbers are hard to spell because there's confusion whether it needs to be the symbol (e.g., "1") or the word (e.g., "one").

5. Try to include a root keyword.

Using men's supplements as an example, including the keyword "supplements" or "men's" somewhere in the domain name will help people find your website much faster. These are chunks of your keyword that are going to be in a lot of search terms people use to find information online.

While it's ideal to include part of your keyword in the domain name, if it goes against all of the previous rules, feel free to forget it. Again, valuable content is more important for your rankings than keywords in your domain name.

6. If you can't find an acceptable ".com" domain name, opt for a ".net" or ".org" suffix.

Runner-ups in the domain suffix race would be ".net" or ".org" suffixes, albeit very distant ones. Suffixes other than the three listed here will be far less desirable. Some regional domain suffixes that are climbing in popularity include ".co," ".nz," and ".uk." Count those regionally specific domain suffixes out because it's going to severely inhibit your ability to rank worldwide.

Helpful Tools for Finding the Best Domain Name

LeanDomainSearch.com: This tool is a domain name generator that takes your keyword and appends prefixes and suffixes to it to generate hundreds or thousands of domain names to choose from. The other neat feature of Lean Domain Search is its ability to check the availability of all the ".com" domain name results generated so you don't have to check each one individually.

This is my absolute favorite tool because it generates good names that may not have immediately come to mind. For example, if I were to search the keyword "tattoo removal," here's what the results would look like:

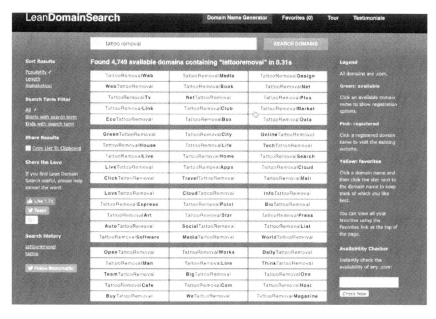

Fig. 04-01
Lean Domain Search results using the search query
"tattoo removal".

All 4,700+ of these ".com" domain names are great options. The results can be sorted alphabetically, by popularity, and length. The "Favorites" feature allows you to keep track of the domain names you like so you don't have to write them down and risk losing track of them.

NameMesh.com: This tool has its uses, but it's not as handy as Lean Domain Search. To contrast, check out this example search result for "tattoo removal:"

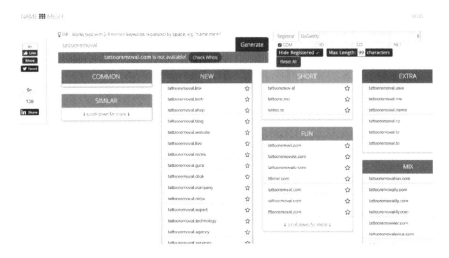

Fig. 04-02
NameMesh.com search results with the search query
"tattoo removal".

As you can see, the domain names generated aren't very usable, but results in the "Common," "Similar," "SEO," and "Mix" columns may serve as inspiration. I'll take this opportunity to reiterate how ineffective domain suffixes other than ".com," ".net," and ".org" are.

NameBoy.com: This is another helpful tool, but, again, not as helpful as Lean Domain Search. Searching for "tattoo" as the primary keyword and "removal" as the secondary keyword would yield the following results:

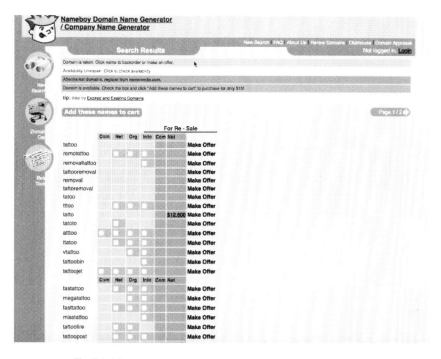

Fig. 04-03
NameBoy search results with the search query "tattoo"
and "removal".

The results generated are an interesting mix between the results from Lean Domain Search and NameMesh.

4.3 Where to Register Your Domain Name

||||||||||||||||||||||||||||||||||||||||||||||||||||||||||||||||||||||||||||||||||||||||||||||||||||

After tinkering with these domain name generators, test them out on actual Domain Name Registrars. A Domain Name Registrar, or Domain Registrar as they're commonly called, is a company that's authorized to register domain names and where you'll buy domain names from.

In this section of Chapter 4 I'm going to outline the pros and cons of each major domain registrar and identify the most cost efficient and convenient options. I'm also going to walk you through buying a domain name.

How and Why I Chose the Domain Name "RueTattoo.com"

Before I dive headfirst into buying a domain name, I'd like to explain the process I went through to get to the domain name for my tattoo removal site to give you an idea of what to expect.

There were two domain names I liked that weren't available: *ThinkBeforeYouInk.com* and *BeforeYouInk.com*. So, after using Lean Domain Search, NameMesh.com, and NameBoy, I landed on the name *TattooRegrets.com*. Unfortunately, that was taken, too.

I then thought *TheDisappearingTattoo.com* or *DisappearingTattoo.com* would have been decent, but I was concerned about the length of the name, and that people would get lost typing it into search engines. A hard lesson to learn in this industry is that your audience isn't as smart as you'd like to give them credit for.

TattooRemovalWeb.com is an exact match keyword I found on Lean Domain Search. Though not very brandable, it would have made a nice choice.

The same goes for *TattooRemovalJournal.com* because if one day I decide to build out this site, the focus will be on my personal experience with the tattoo removal process. While either of these names would have been workable, I didn't love them.

So, the next concept I landed on was *TattooRegrets.com*. Not really loving it, I searched synonyms for the word "regret" in Google and one of the results was the word "rue." I really liked that word and decided on the domain name *RueTattoo.com*.

Yes, there's potential for misspelling, but it's short, contains a root keyword, and shares a double meaning: "rue" is French for "street," so it's like saying "Tattoo Street." *RueTattoo.com* is an example of a domain name that doesn't check all the boxes and isn't perfect, but it's close.

The Best Place to Register Domain Names

Registering a domain name is more complex than most people think; it's not as simple as clicking a button. That's why I'm going to outline the process in the next few sections. The three major options for registering a domain are:

1. The hosting company

2. GoDaddy.com

3. Namecheap.com

GoDaddy.com and *Namecheap.com* are just two of the dozens, if not hundreds, of domain registrars that exist, but these are the two most common domain registrars in the Internet Marketing community. The main difference between these three options is cost, and one of the factors that adds to the cost is domain privacy.

Domain privacy is a service offered by most domain name registrars when you purchase a domain name. If you register a domain name and *don't* opt for domain privacy, all of your registration information is open to the public: full name, home or company address, phone number, and email. Personally, I'm not too comfortable with this information being available to everyone, and you shouldn't be either. My recommendation is to always purchase domain privacy.

The Easy Option: The Hosting Company

If you register a domain name with a registrar that's not your hosting company, you'll have to connect the domain name and said registrar by updating your name servers. If that sounds really technical, that's because it is. So, if you'd prefer to avoid this step, you can simply register your domain with your hosting company.

The disadvantage of registering with your hosting company is that it's going to cost an extra $10 to $12 a year. Now, this might not mean a lot if you're building a single website, but you'll probably own a lot of domains if you plan to stick it out in Internet Marketing.

It's worth noting that this seemingly complicated and technical step takes five minutes, tops. That means you're paying an extra $10 a year to save five minutes of your time. Personally, I don't recommend this option.

The Short-Term Cheap Option: GoDaddy

Most people default to GoDaddy because they are well-known, have decent upfront pricing, and run incredible promotions. GoDaddy also provides domain names for as low as $1 for the first year and $3 for the first year of a ".com" domain (plus privacy). Pretty sweet, huh?

The problem with GoDaddy, though, is the long-term pricing. After the first year, expect the price to spike to about $25 a year (they have to make their money back somehow). That price has been going up over the years, yet there's not enough added value to justify it.

The Long-Term Simple, Mainstream, and Cheap Option: Namecheap

Namecheap is another popular choice for domain registry. The difference between Namecheap and GoDaddy is that Namecheap ends up being cheaper in the end. The baseline pricing starts at $10 to $11 a year, especially if you have a coupon code for the first year.

Namecheap also charges the lowest price for domain privacy; it's included *for free* during the first year. After that, the price is $3 a year, whereas GoDaddy charges 10% or more. Hosting companies typically charge somewhere between $10 to $12 a year for domain privacy. For these reasons, Namecheap is my personal choice.

4.4 Securing Hosting for Your Website

In this section of chapter 4, I'm going to outline another essential component of your website: **hosting**. You'll learn what **shared hosting** is, the best place to host your website, and why you should invest in **unlimited domains**.

What Is Hosting?

Hosting is a service that companies provide to website owners. Simply put, hosting companies provide storage space and access for websites through the use of **web servers**, or computers that specifically store files that comprise websites.

The hosting company sells a specific amount of storage space, as well as access to that space, to website owners to store their files. Every time you fire up your internet browser and type in a website's URL, your browser is accessing files from that website's host server and displaying it to you.

What Is Shared Hosting?

Shared hosting means you're sharing server space with a lot of other websites. This is the most basic service that a hosting company will provide, and the one you'll start with. In time, when you reach a certain level of traffic, you can move to a **virtual private server** for improved performance, and eventually move to a **dedicated server**, where your website is the only one using that server. Dedicated servers make it possible for websites to load faster, and usually have additional features that improve your website's security and performance. Don't worry about that right now, though; that's months or years away.

Why I Recommend Bluehost

There are hundreds of different hosting companies to choose from, and over the years, I've purchased hosting from over a dozen different companies. I've hosted with every single one of the absolute

4.4 SECURING HOSTING FOR YOUR WEBSITE

best brands available and I've had varying experiences with each. I've had experiences that were bad enough to make me never register or host my websites with that company again.

Bluehost has the best service and support over any other low-cost shared hosting company I've worked with, particularly because **they've <u>very</u> deliberately gone out of their way to help FIMP community members.** Based on my experience, they're the best **value** hosting company for beginners/mid-stage website owners.

Are they the best hosting company ever? **Absolutely not.** But they're the perfect combination of value, quality, and service until you're getting at least a few hundred visitors to your website per day.

NOTE: This is not at all required, but... if you're signing up for hosting and you wouldn't mind supporting what we're doing at FIMP, please consider purchasing through our link at https://stoppingscams.com/FIMP/links-and-resources/.

It won't cost you anything extra (we've actually negotiated the best discounts possible), but these commissions help FIMP tremendously — and we have a lot of bonus content and community support that we'll set you up with as a "thank you!"

Don't feel remotely obligated or pressured, but it would help our project and community more than *words can say if you find the contents of this book and the video training at FIMP helpful.*

Why You Should Sign Up for Unlimited Domains

For now, you're going to be signing up for a single domain, but you're going to want to pay slightly more for unlimited domains; this will make your experience much easier down the road. Whether you register another domain two weeks from now and start a different site or abandon the niche you're working in and want to host another site two months from now, you're eventually going to need it.

How to Sign Up with Bluehost

Note: If watching this in action is more helpful, you can purchase access to the step-by-step video version of this training at https:// stoppingscams. com/FIMP/.

When you click on the "Get Started" button from the Bluehost.com homepage, you'll be routed to the pricing page where you can choose from one of three hosting tiers: **Basic**, **Plus**, or **Prime**.

The **Basic** hosting tier offers hosting for one domain. The **Plus** tier offers hosting for unlimited websites. Although you get one domain for free, it's best to host the first domain with Namecheap because only the first year is free with Bluehost.

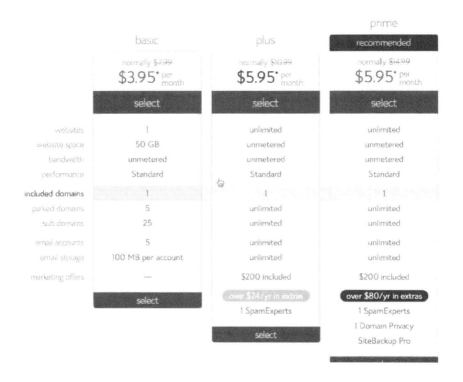

Fig. 04-04 - Bluehost hosting tiers: Basic, Plus, and Prime.

Fig. 04-05 - Bluehost's Plus Plan inclusions and upsells.

It's going to be more expensive, at around $25 per year, after the first year.

The **Prime** tier offers domain privacy for your domains, which you won't need to get from Bluehost if you registered your domain name with Namecheap (you can get domain privacy from them).

Clicking on the "Select" button under any of the hosting tiers will route you to a page where you can enter a domain name. After entering a domain name, you're routed to the checkout page where you can select a tier and the duration of the service.

At the checkout page, **make sure to uncheck any upsells before completing your order**. Site Backup Pro, Search Engine Jumpstart, and SiteLock Security are unnecessary at this point and provide little to no value.

Once you enter all the necessary information and check out, you'll immediately receive a payment confirmation to your email inbox. There's a waiting period involved while Bluehost sets up your hosting; once that's done, you'll receive an additional email with vital information. Print that email and mark it as important in your email account because it contains important information you'll likely need while you're with Bluehost.

Congratulations! You've signed up for hosting with Bluehost!

4.5 Linking Your Domain Name and Hosting Account

Note: If you acquired a domain name with a hosting provider, you can skip this section.

At this point, you should already have a domain name registered and a hosting account secured, which means you're ready to link the two.

Updating Your Nameservers

Your domain is essentially your web address that people use to find your website on the internet, and your hosting server houses your website files. What we're trying to do is connect the two so that when people type your domain name in their browser and click "Go," the browser knows where to retrieve your website files to display them.

To connect your domain and hosting server you need to update the **nameservers** in your domain registrar. The nameservers that need to be placed in your domain registrar are provided by your hosting provider. So, in our case, updating the nameservers in Namecheap tells it to connect to your website hosted by Bluehost when someone types in your domain name.

This is why you can skip this step if you registered your domain with your hosting provider; the nameservers are already pointing to the right place. If you acquired them separately, however, you'll need to connect them.

Updating Namecheap with Nameservers from Bluehost

Different domain registrars have different ways to update their nameservers. Similarly, different hosting providers have different nameservers. So, if you didn't opt for Namecheap and/or Bluehost, now is the time to Google what company you opted for because I won't be discussing all of them here (it's quite impossible to do given how many domain registrars and hosting providers there are).

Note: the process I'll be outlining in this section is for a website whose domain name is registered to Namecheap and is hosted by Bluehost.

The first step is to log into your Namecheap account. When you log in, you'll be redirected to this page. Next, click on the tab titled "Domain List" on the left.

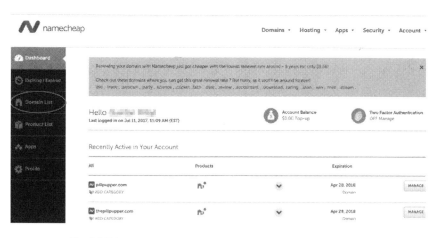

Fig. 04-06
Namecheap Dashboard with "Domain List" highlighted.

You'll be routed to a page that lists your various domains. Next, click on the "Manage" button for the intended domain.

Fig. 04-07
Namecheap Domain List with "Manage" highlighted.

You'll be routed a page that displays the details of your domain. In the "nameservers" section click on the dropdown menu. Then, click the option "Custom DNS."

Fig. 04-08
Namecheap Manage Domain with "Nameservers" and "Custom DNS" highlighted.

Once you select "Custom DNS," two blank spaces will appear. Input the following:

- ns1.bluehost.com
- ns2.bluehost.com

Here's what that should look like:

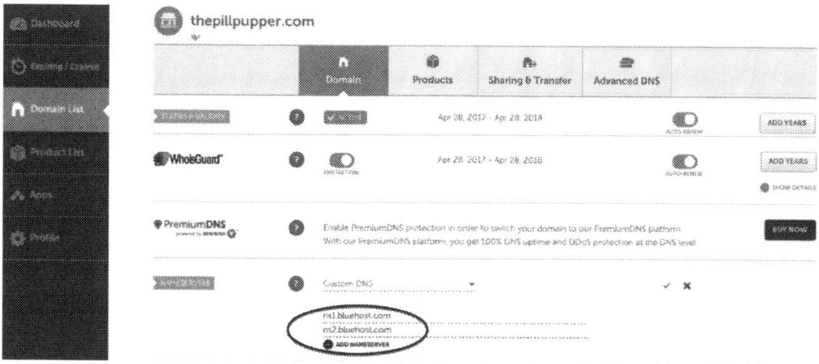

Fig. 04-09
Namecheap Manage Domain Custom DNS fields filled
out with Bluehost nameservers.

Bluehost designates the same nameservers for everyone, so there's no need to log in to your Bluehost account to do all this.

Note that you don't need to click on "Add Nameservers" below the fields. After inputting each Custom DNS, click on the green check-mark next to the "Custom DNS" dropdown menu. Once you've completed this last step wait a few seconds to ensure everything went through, and then you're done!

That wasn't so bad, was it?

It's important to note that it could take anywhere from 10 minutes to 48 hours for the changes to be applied.

Again, if you have a different registrar or if you have a different hosting company, just Google how to update the nameservers. You'll probably find a YouTube video or a step-by-step guide with screenshots from either your hosting company or domain registrar detailing how to do it.

4.6 Why WordPress Is the Only Platform You Should Use

Before you can get your website to work, you'll need a platform to build your website on, such as a Content Management System (CMS). There are many options available, from the tried-and-tested to the done-for-you. However, one CMS stands out among the rest: **WordPress**. In this section of Chapter 4, I'll discuss why WordPress is the ONLY platform you should consider using.

Admittedly, there are easier CMS platforms to learn than WordPress, like SquareSpace, Weebly, and Wix, to name a few. However, their ease of use is also their biggest disadvantage. There will be a point in your Internet Marketing business where you'll need to customize things that these done-for-you platforms either bury deep in their code or restrict access to. Even when you try to find solutions and workarounds, there are too few users of these platforms. That means not all the solutions are readily available.

WordPress has so many users that it's likely someone has experienced the same difficulties you might encounter and posted about them. It's the same story for any custom functions you want to place on your website; chances are someone somewhere has tried it and either posted how to do it or posted why it can't be done.

Another reason to opt for WordPress is their **plugin** selection. Plugins are little pieces of software that add various functions to your website. Although plugins are available for other platforms, WordPress' selection is unrivaled in terms of number, variety, and quality. If you ever hope to build a profitable internet business, WordPress is the way to go.

For more details comparing the different CMS platforms available, their pros and cons, and why WordPress is hands-down the best platform, read my article titled *How to Build a Blog from Scratch: A Comprehensive Guide* on https://stoppingscams.com/.

4.7 How to Install WordPress in Less Than Five Minutes

The next step to building your website is installing a CMS. Since I've established that WordPress is the best CMS, that's what I'm going to recommend you install for your Bluehost hosted websites.

Three Scenarios to Cover

Scenario 1 means you bought your domain at Bluehost.

Scenario 2 means you bought your domain with another registrar (i.e., Namecheap, GoDaddy, etc.) AND signed up for Bluehost using this domain.

Scenario 3 means you bought your domain with another registrar AND signed up for Bluehost, but you didn't use that domain to sign up with Bluehost.

Scenario 1: Bought Domain at Bluehost

By default, WordPress is installed once Bluehost gets your account set up, so **you don't need to do anything else**.

Scenario 2: Bought Domain with Another Registrar AND Signed Up for Bluehost with That Domain

In this scenario, you bought your domain with another registrar (in our example, it's Namecheap) and then used that to sign up for Bluehost. This is what it looks like:

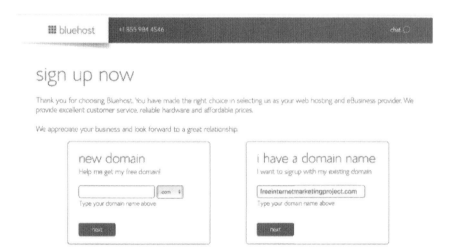

Fig. 04-10
Bluehost Sign Up page with option "I have a domain name"
filled out and selected.

If you input your domain name in the "I have a domain name" section and clicked "Next," AND if you followed the steps in section 4.5 correctly (i.e., updated your Nameservers with your Domain Registrar), then WordPress has already been installed. **You don't need to do anything else.**

You can check that your nameservers have been updated by logging in to your Bluehost account. Then, go to "My Sites" on the left-hand side of the page. Hover the mouse over your domain and click on "Manage Site." Here's what it looks like:

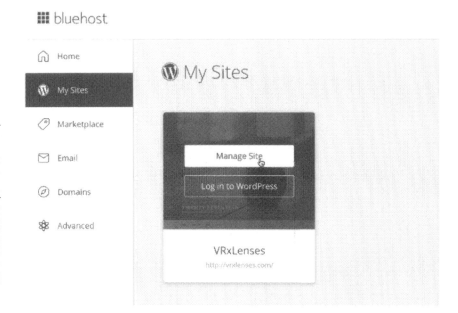

Fig. 04-11
Bluehost My Sites with "Manage Site" highlighted.

You'll be routed to the "Manage Site" page. Click on "Settings" in the navigation menu and check that the URL under "Site URL" is your actual domain.

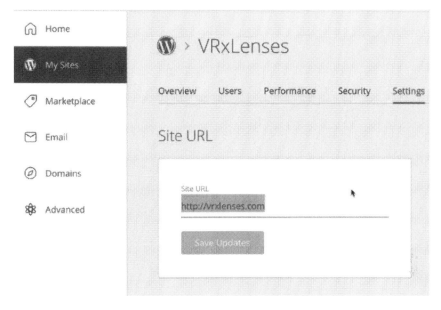

Fig. 04-12
Bluehost Manage Site with "Settings" selected and "Site
URL" highlighted.

*Note: This process is
also covered, step-
by-step, in the video
version of this training.
Purchase access
today at https://
stoppingscams.com/
FIMP/.*

Scenario 3: Bought Domain with Another Registrar AND Signed Up for Bluehost But Didn't Use That Domain to Sign Up with Bluehost

As you can probably guess, this is the most complicated scenario to deal with. This applies if you
bought your domain through another registrar,
but you did NOT sign up during the Bluehost process. Either you forgot to use the domain when

you were setting up Bluehost, you didn't have a domain yet when you set up Bluehost, or you plan to buy another domain down the road and you want to create that website on the same Bluehost hosting account.

Here's an overview of the steps that need to be completed:

1. Update nameservers (refer to Section 4.5) with domain registrar.

2. Create an Addon Domain in the Bluehost cPanel.

3. Install WordPress for new domain.

4. Double-check website to ensure correct URL set up.

Before anything else, you need to update your nameservers with your domain registrar. The following process will not work if your nameservers aren't updated.

Once that's sorted out, you need to log in to your Bluehost account. Then, click on the "Domains" tab on the left-hand side of the page to display a new page. Then, you need to click on "Assign a domain to your cPanel account." Here's what it looks like:

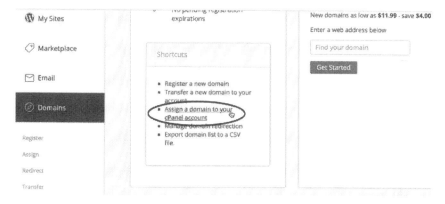

Fig. 04-13
Bluehost Domains with "Assign a domain to your cPanel
account" clicked.

That will take you to another screen. Select "Use a
domain that is not already associated with your account" and input your domain in the "Domain" field.

Fig. 04-14
Bluehost, assign a domain to your cPanel account,
Step 1: Enter Domain. Select "Use a domain that is not
already associated with your account."

4.7 HOW TO INSTALL WORDPRESS IN LESS THAN FIVE MINUTES

Once you've input your domain and it's been ver-ified, a confirmation message that your domain has been verified will be displayed.

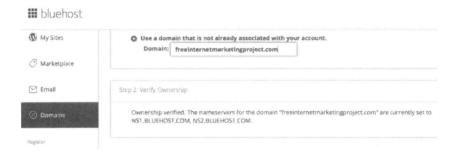

Fig. 04-15
Bluehost, assign a domain to your cPanel account, Step 2:
Verify Ownership. Note the confirmation message that
domain has been verified.

The next step is to make sure the "Addon Domain" option is selected.

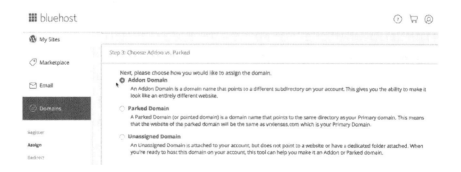

Fig. 04-16
Bluehost, assign a domain to your cPanel account, Step 3:
Choose Addon vs. Parked. Select "Addon Domain."

Next, make sure that the "Create a new directory" button is selected.

Fig. 04-17
Bluehost, assign a domain to your cPanel account, Step 4:
Choose Addon Directory and Sub-domain. Select "Create
a new directory."

When all of these steps are complete, you can then click "Assign this Domain" near the bottom of the page.

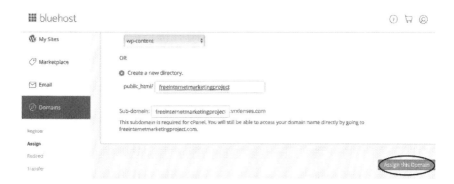

Fig. 04-18
Bluehost, assign a domain to your cPanel account, "Assign
this Domain" button.

Once processed and done, your site should be listed in the "Domains" page as an Addon Domain.

Fig. 04-19

Bluehost's Domains page. Note that the created addon domain from the previous step is displayed.

Now that we've created an Addon domain, we can now install WordPress to that domain.

To do that, you'll need to click on "My Sites" on the left-hand side of the page, then the blue "Create Site" button in the upper right corner of the page.

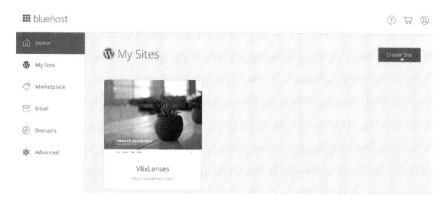

Fig. 04-20
Bluehost's "My Sites" page with "Create Site" button.

Clicking "Create Site" will route you to the "Create a new WordPress site" page where you'll be asked to input your Site Name and Site Tagline. Don't stress about this too much at this point because you can easily change that in the future.

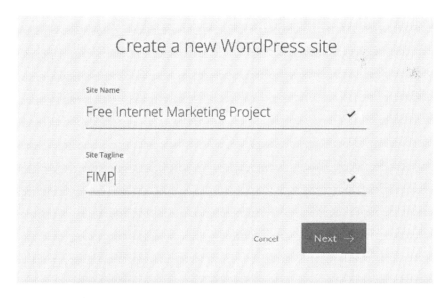

Fig. 04-21
Bluehost's "Create a new WordPress Site" page. Take note of the required information (Site Name and Site Tagline).

4.7 HOW TO INSTALL WORDPRESS IN LESS THAN FIVE MINUTES

Once you've input a Site Name and Sit Tagline, click on "Next" to be taken to the "Choose a Domain" page. Make sure you select the correct domain under the "Domain" dropdown menu. If you select the wrong domain, you'll overwrite the existing WordPress installation on that domain. Leave the space under Directory blank and uncheck the boxes for "WP Forms" and "Opt-in Monster."

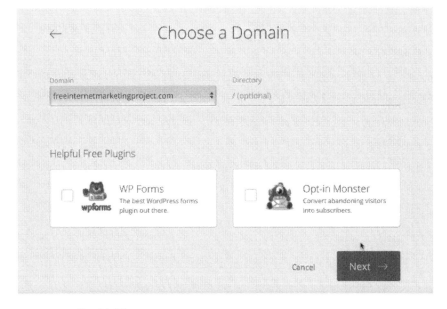

Fig. 04-22
Bluehost's "Choose a Domain" page. Make sure to select
the correct domain under the "Domain" dropdown menu
and not to enter anything under "Directory."

It will take a few seconds to a few minutes for WordPress to set up. Once complete, a confirmation page will be displayed with important login details, such as the WordPress Admin page and your username and password. This information will also be sent to the registered email address.

Fig. 04-23

Bluehost's WordPress installation confirmation page.

WordPress should now be installed on your domain. You can check it by logging into your WordPress account or simply going to the domain through your browser.

 If you encounter any technical issues during set up, contact Bluehost. If you're not in the U.S., you can relay difficulties to Bluehost via their Support Team Twitter account (*@bluehostsupport*).

4.8 Stripping All of the Default Crap from WordPress

Now that you've installed WordPress you're ready to strip the default settings. You might be wondering, "why bother?"

The purpose of the default post and page are to show what they look like on your theme. These are unnecessary and may cause confusion down the line. Also, some plugins that are installed by default have been around for a while, and there are much better versions available now. Some of them can even slow down your website, which isn't a good thing.

The first step is to delete the sample page and sample post along with sample comments. Log in to WordPress to access your Dashboard. Then, click on "Posts" on the left-hand side of the page, and then click "All Posts" to see the sample post.

Fig. 04-24
WordPress Dashboard, "Posts" page.

The sample post is titled, "Hello World!" Click "Trash" under the post title to delete both the post and its sample comments.

Next, click on "Pages" on the left-hand side of the page, and then click "All Pages" to see the sample page. To delete the sample page, click "Trash" under the page title.

Fig. 04-25
WordPress Dashboard, "Pages" page.

Next, you need to click "Plugins" on the left-hand side of the page to display the plugins that are included with your WordPress installation. Most of these have to go because they're outdated or unnecessary at this stage.

Fig. 04-26
WordPress Dashboard, "Plugins" page.

I recommend deleting the following plugins:

- Akismet Anti-Spam

- Hello Dolly

- Jetpack by WordPress.com

- MOJO Marketplace

- Optin Monster API

- WPForms Lite

4.9 Setting Your Business Up for Profit in WordPress

Now that you've stripped WordPress of all of the useless crap, it's time to set up things in their place that are actually helpful for your business. I'm going to walk you through installing necessary plugins and adjusting a handful of settings to ensure your business will be profitable in the coming months as you add content.

Making WordPress as Hassle-Free as Possible

We want to achieve a couple of things here:

First, we want your site to be optimized for search engines. This is part of a very basic aspect of Search Engine Optimization (SEO). We're merely setting the stage for further optimization down the road.

Second, we need to address WordPress' security vulnerabilities. If your site gets hacked, you could lose access to your site. Someone could infect your files with a virus. Worst, someone could delete your entire website. Now is a good time to address security.

Installing Essential Plugins and Setting Site Structure

The essential plugins that we're going to install are:

- Yoast SEO - helps make your site SEO friendly.

- Easy Updates Manager - handles updates for WordPress, plugins, and themes.

- Wordfence - aids with the security of your site.

- Contact Form 7 - allows the setup of customizable contact forms on your site.

Regarding site structure, we're going to adjust your site's **permalink structure** as well as the **nickname** that's publicly displayed.

Permalinks are the permanent URLs assigned to your blog posts, as well as other pages of your blog. We're going to adjust *how* your permalinks are structured because search engines use these URLs to index your site. These permalinks need to be SEO friendly.

I recommend changing your nickname because this is displayed publicly. WordPress sets your nickname to be the same as your username by default. For security purposes, you want the username not to be known by everyone because if a determined hacker gets hold of your username, they can try and access your WordPress dashboard by guessing your password.

Installing and Setting Up Yoast SEO

From the WordPress Dashboard, click "Plugins" on the left-hand side, and then click "Add New." That will take you to the "Add Plugins" page. Type the word "yoast" in the search field located in the upper right-hand corner. Yoast SEO will be the first search result. Next, click "Install Now" to install the plugin.

Fig. 04-27
WordPress Dashboard, "Add Plugins" page. Note that Yoast SEO is displayed as the first result when "yoast" is searched.

Note: This installation process is the same for all other plugins.

Once Yoast SEO is installed, the "Install Now" button turns into the "Activate" button. Click on that button. This action will navigate to the Plugins page.

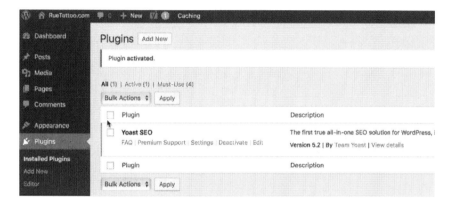

Fig. 04-28
WordPress Dashboard, "Plugins page" with confirmation message that Yoast SEO was activated.

Now that Yoast SEO has been installed, it needs to be set up.

Notice that you have a new menu item on the left-hand side called "SEO" with the Yoast SEO logo. Hover over the "SEO" menu option, and then click on the "General" menu option to access the Yoast SEO Dashboard.

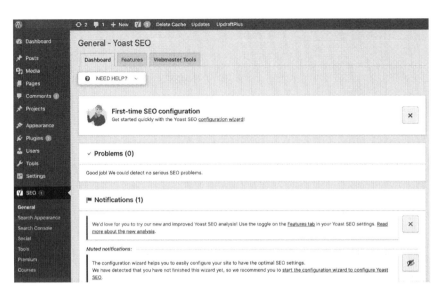

Fig. 04-29
WordPress Dashboard and Yoast SEO Dashboard.

You can choose to enable or disable features to assist the SEO of your site (depending on what you'll actually use) in the "Features" tab of the Yoast SEO Dashboard. You don't want to enable features that won't be used because they're using resources on your server and possibly slowing down your website.

For example, I never pay attention to the readability analysis. The readability analysis can slow down how quickly you're able to type in the editor if you're writing long posts (around 3,000 words or more).

Next, click on the "Search Appearance" menu option. You can access this by hovering over the

"SEO" menu option on the left. Then, click to the "Taxonomies" tab and scroll down to the "Tags" section. **Look for the slide switch titled "Show Tags in search results?" and switch it to "no."** Scroll down to the bottom and click "Save changes."

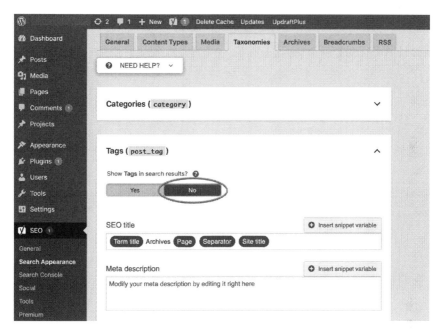

Fig. 04-30
WordPress Dashboard, Yoast SEO "Search Appearance"
page, "Taxonomies" tab, "Tags" section, "Show Tags in
search results" set to "Yes" by default. Switch this to "No."

The same procedure needs to be performed for another type of page. Click on the "Archives" tab from the "Search Appearance" page and scroll down to the "Author archives settings." **Look for** the slide switch titled **"Show author archives in search results?" and switch it to "no."** Scroll down to the bottom and click "Save changes."

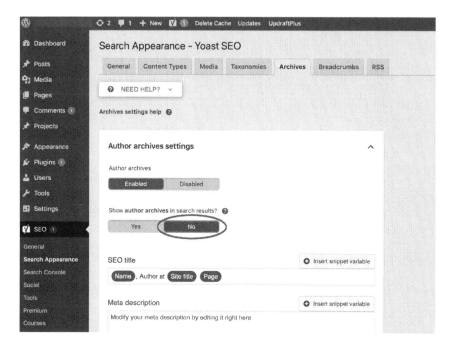

Fig. 04-31
WordPress Dashboard, Yoast SEO "Search Appearance" page, "Archives" tab, "Author archives settings" section, "Show author archives in search results" set to "Yes" by default. Switch this to "No."

What you've just done is change the settings of the Tags and Author archives pages so that they're not saved by search engine databases, something known as being **indexed**.

A Note About Indexing

Indexing and **ranking** are two very different things. If a page or post is indexed, that doesn't mean it will be on the first page of search results. If a page is indexed, that means the page is now in search engines' databases, particularly Google, and people can find that page through Google.com. If the Tags and Author archives pages are allowed to be indexed, they can compete and even outrank your actual blog posts in search engine results.

Having Tags and Author archives pages indexed isn't ideal because they're basically a collection of posts. It's better to show people your blog posts with helpful content. By electing to not show Tags or author archives in search results, you just told search engines to not include your Tags and Author archives pages in their database because those are fairly worthless pages that compete against pages and posts you actually want to rank.

This might not make much sense to you right now if you've never dealt with SEO before but keep it in mind as you move forward.

All the other Yoast SEO settings don't matter too much. If you want to research and explore some of them, you certainly can, but if you don't want to adjust anything else you can move on to the next section.

Installing and Setting Up Easy Updates Manager

The next plugin we're going to install and update is Easy Updates Manager. The installation is very similar to the installation process for Yoast SEO:

- Plugins → Add New → type "Easy Updates Manager" in the search field → click "Install Now" → click "Activate."

Fig. 04-32
WordPress Dashboard, "Add Plugins" page. Note that Easy Updates Manager is displayed as the first result when "easy updates manager" is searched.

Once Easy Updates Manager has been activated, you'll be routed to the Plugins page (see Fig. 04-33).

Unlike Yoast SEO, a new menu option will not appear in the left-hand menu. To set up Easy Updates Manager or to change any of the existing settings, you'll need to navigate to the Plugins page and click "Configure" below its name: "Easy Updates Manager." This action will navigate to the Easy Updates Manager Dashboard.

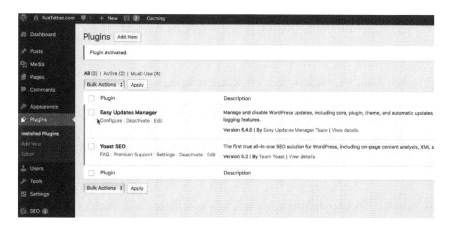

Fig. 04-33

*WordPress Dashboard, "Plugins page" with confirmation
message that Easy Updates Manager was activated.*

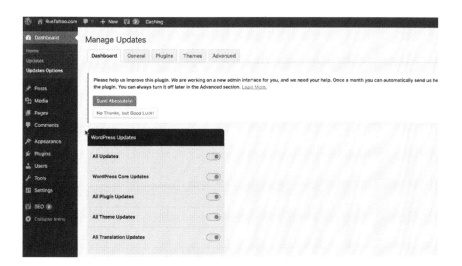

Fig. 04-34

*WordPress Dashboard, Easy Updates Manager
Dashboard, WordPress "Updates" section with all
updates turned on by default. Leave these settings as is.*

By default, all WordPress updates are turned on, which is what you want. Scroll down to the "Automatic Updates" section. Turn on "Major Releases" and leave "Development Updates" turned off.

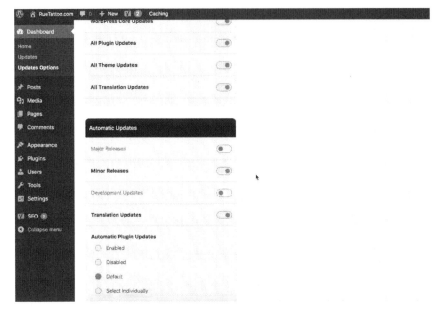

Fig. 04-35
WordPress Dashboard, Easy Updates Manager Dashboard, "Automatic Updates" section. Turn on updates for "Major Releases" and leave "Development Updates" turned off.

Scroll further down and enable "Automatic Plugin Updates" and "Automatic Theme Updates" (see Fig. 04-36).

Further down, there's the "Plugin and Theme Updates" section. There you can change settings for individual plugins and themes, but it's best to have them all turned on.

Fig. 04-36
WordPress Dashboard, Easy Updates Manager Dashboard,
"Automatic Updates" section with "Automatic Plugin
Updates" and "Automatic Theme Updates" radio buttons.
Enable both updates.

All of the changes made for the latest version of this plugin are automatically saved. There's no need to click a save button.

By installing and setting up the Easy Updates Manager plugin you've created a second layer of protection in the event the Bluehost default automatic updates fail. WordPress security is something to take very seriously and keeping your site and its components updated is a big part of having a secure website.

Installing and Setting Up Wordfence Security

Wordfence Security is my plugin of choice because it's one of the leading security plugins for WordPress.

Once again, the installation is very similar to the previous installation processes:

- Plugins → Add New → type "Wordfence" in the search field → click "Install Now" → click "Activate."

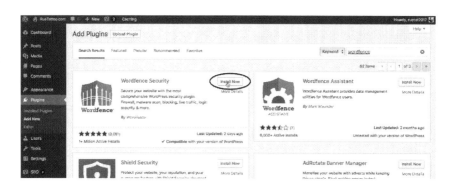

Fig. 04-37
WordPress Dashboard, "Add Plugins" page. Note that
Wordfence Security is displayed as the first result when
"Wordfence" is searched.

Once Wordfence Security has been activated, you'll be routed to the Plugins page (see Fig. 04-38).

Now that Wordfence is installed, it's time to set it up.

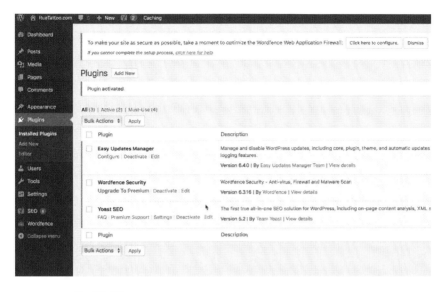

Fig. 04-38
WordPress Dashboard, "Plugins" page with confirmation
message that Wordfence Security was activated. Note
new menu option on the left-hand side of the page titled
"Wordfence" with the Wordfence logo.

Notice the new menu item on the left-hand side titled "Wordfence" with the Wordfence logo; click it, and then click "Dashboard."

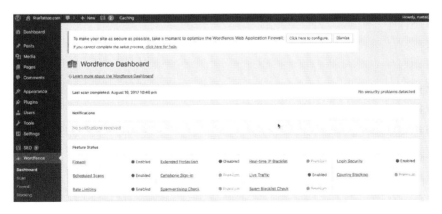

Fig. 04-39
WordPress Dashboard, Wordfence Security Dashboard.

From experience, Wordfence's default settings are more than good enough to help protect your site, so we're going to leave them as they are. If you're interested in learning more about these settings, Google and study them since I won't be going into detail.

To check that the Wordfence Web Application Firewall is set up correctly, scroll up to the field that states: *"To make your site as secure as possible, take a moment to optimize the Wordfence Web Application Firewall."*

Then, click the link that states, "Click here to configure."

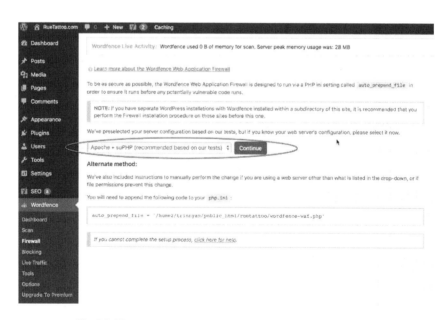

Fig. 04-40
WordPress Dashboard, Wordfence Security, "Web Application Firewall" page. Make sure that "Apache + suPHP" is selected.

From the dropdown menu, select "Apache + suPHP" then click "Continue" (see Fig. 04-40).

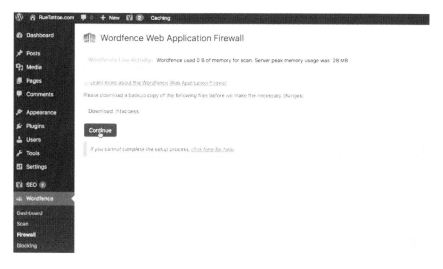

Fig. 04-41
WordPress Dashboard, Wordfence Security, "Web
Application Firewall" page, "Download .htaccess" option.

A "Download .htaccess" option will appear - click on it. Explaining the purpose of .htaccess is for a more advanced lesson. For now, just know that .htaccess is an important WordPress file that contains installation configuration settings. There will be times when the installation or configuration of something new will mess up the WordPress site. Having a backup of the current version of the .htaccess file may help fix any issues when uploaded again. Downloading the .htaccess file is a precaution to take when installing or setting up something that can break your site. It's not a cure-all; the safest backup is a backup of your WordPress installation (an advanced lesson).

Once the .htaccess file is downloaded, click "Continue" to proceed.

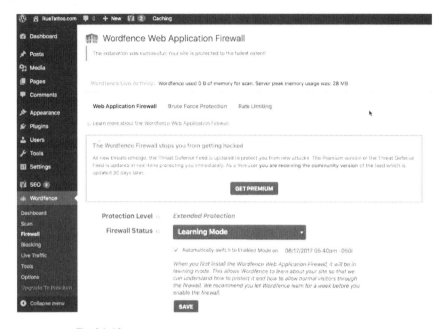

Fig. 04-42

WordPress Dashboard, Wordfence Security, "Web Application Firewall" page with confirmation message that the Web Application Firewall has been successfully installed. Note that the Firewall Status is "Learning Mode," which is what we want.

Wordfence Security should now be successfully set up for your WordPress site.

Installing and Setting Up Contact Form 7

Once again, the installation of Contact Form 7 is very similar to the previous installation processes:

- Plugins → Add New → type "contact form" in the search field → click "Install Now" → click "Activate."

I don't really have a strict preference for contact forms. Contact Form 7 is highly rated and updated frequently. Try to get in the habit of looking for highly rated plugins that are updated frequently.

Contact Form 7 creates its own menu option in the left-hand menu titled "Contact" when installed.

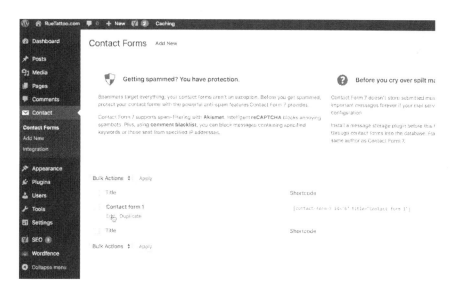

Fig. 04-43
WordPress Dashboard, Contact Form 7, "Contact Forms" page with "Contact form 1" displayed.

"Contact form 1" is the default form in this plugin. You can make changes to it by clicking on "Edit" directly below the name on the "Contact Forms" page.

Clicking on "Edit" will navigate to a page where contact forms can be customized. At the moment it should look like code: it describes what people would see whenever "Contact form 1" is embedded in a page.

Fig. 04-44
WordPress Dashboard, Contact Form 7, "Edit Contact Form" page for Contact form 1, "Form" tab.

For example, when "Contact form 1" is embedded in a page, four fields will appear:

- "Your Name (required)"
- "Your Email (required)"
- "Subject"
- "Your Message"

At the bottom there will be a button titled "Send" that submits the completed form to an email address when clicked.

To change *where* the completed form is sent, click "Mail" and change the default WordPress admin email to the email address you want to receive completed forms. For example, my default WordPress admin email is "ian@stoppingscams.com," so I'd want to update it to "ian@ruetattoo.com."

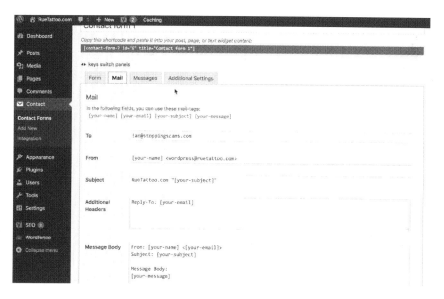

Fig. 04-45
WordPress Dashboard, Contact Form 7, "Edit Contact Form" for Contact form 1, "Mail" tab.

You can basically change the email address to whatever email address you prefer. For my example tattoo site, my preference is ian@ruetattoo.com because it shares the same domain and is more official.

The rest of the fields adjust the settings for how fields will appear in your email. For example, if we leave the rest of the fields as is, any time a visitor fills out "Contact form 1" on a page, you'll receive an email with the following information:

- From:
  [the name entered in the "Your Name" field]

- Subject:
  [the subject entered in the "Subject" field]

- Reply-To:
  [the email entered in the "Your Email" field]

- The Message Body, which contains all of the above information plus the message entered in the "Your Message" field

As with most plugins, you can do a Google search on how to tweak the settings, especially if you want additional information from those who will be filling out your form. Remember that you can set up another contact form that asks for a different set of information.

Setting Up Your Permalink Structure

Permalink structure needs to be set up correctly for SEO purposes. I'll discuss SEO in more detail in the next few chapters, but right now your keywords need to be both in the title of your post *and* in the post URL, which is its Permalink. If you set up the permalink structure correctly, the post title will automatically be in your permalink and you won't have to adjust it every time you publish a post.

First, you need to navigate to "Settings" in the left-hand menu, then click "Permalinks."

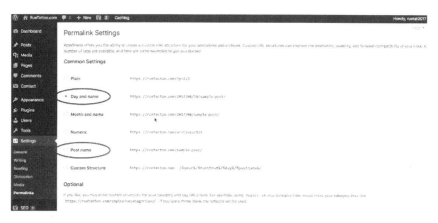

Fig. 04-46
WordPress Dashboard, Settings, "Permalink Settings"
page with default permalink structure "Day and name"
selected. Make sure to change it to "Post name."

The default structure is "Day and name," so we need to change it to "Post name." Then, click "Save changes" at the bottom of the page. And you're done!

Setting Up Displayed User Profile

By default, WordPress sets your displayed name as your username. For security reasons, I don't want the world to know the username I use to log in, and you shouldn't, either. If someone knows your username, they're that much closer to hacking your website, so take care of it. I don't want the world to know my last name, either. That's up to you, of course, but I would advise not to publish your last name as well.

To change these settings in WordPress, navigate to and click "Users" in the left-hand menu. Then, click on "All Users" to display all the usernames connected to your WordPress account. If you only have one account, the only username displayed will be the first one you set up, which is the one you use to log in to WordPress.

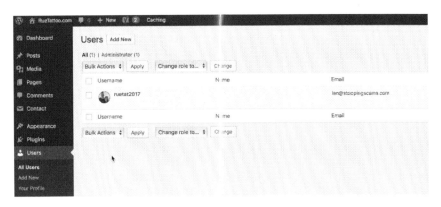

Fig. 04-47
WordPress Dashboard, "Users" page with the username displayed.

Clicking "Edit" below the username will navigate to the Profile page. Scroll down to the "Name" section.

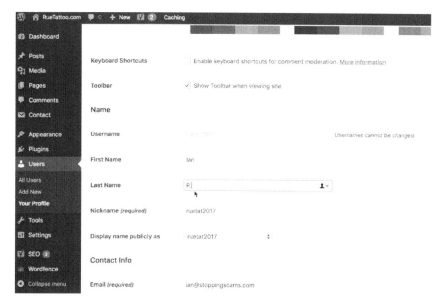

Fig. 04-48
WordPress Dashboard, "Users" page, Profile Page, "Name" section. Note that the "Display name publicly as" field has the username by default. After you input a First Name, Last Name, and Nickname, the "Display name publicly as" field will become a dropdown menu that will show other choices such as "First Name, Last Name," "First Name + Last Name," and "Nickname."

By default, the "First Name" and "Last Name" fields are blank, while the "Nickname" and "Display name publicly as" fields are populated with your username. Fill out the "First Name," "Last Name," and "Nickname" fields so the "Display name publicly as" field will display more options. After setting a Nickname, it's available to select from a dropdown menu as the display name. The display name you choose is up to you. You can also choose to change the email address.

How to display a profile picture is beyond the scope of this lesson, and an unnecessary step. If that's something you choose to do, set up a Gravatar account for that email address. Do a Google search to learn more about how to display a profile picture on WordPress.

When you're done, click "Update" at the bottom of the page.

4.10 Choosing Your Theme and Crucial Design Tips

When using WordPress, the chosen theme heavily dictates your website design. I want to outline some crucial design tips, especially for beginners in this industry, to create a profitable website as quickly as possible.

Pick Your Battles

Before thinking about a theme, website design, and all the aesthetics, I want to make an important point about what your mindset should be.

As you set out to create a profitable Internet Marketing business, you will find that you're about to encounter dozens of battles over the next several months. It's very important that you pick your battles wisely.

Sadly, a battle many people pick very early on, including myself, is website appearance and design. Design doesn't matter until traffic is consistent, and to start getting traffic, all you need design-wise is a simple website that's easy to navigate and mobile-responsive.

For now, the focus should be on traffic-producing activities, such as high-quality content. Every second spent thinking about unnecessary design elements is a second taken away from producing high-quality content, and that's time taken away from generating traffic, which means delaying your success.

Design Elements That Matter Right Now

If you're just starting out, the only things that matter, in terms of website design, are that your website is clean, easy to navigate, and mobile responsive – THAT'S IT.

As you create content and optimize it for search engines, there will be other elements to bear in mind.

However, the ones mentioned above are all that matter right now. When selecting a theme, make sure it has all three.

Examples of elements that aren't important at this stage and can be added or changed later are **image headers** and **website colors** (or color combinations). Too many people become stuck when they get started struggling to figure out the background or font color. Spending time on aesthetics at this point is a waste of time. There are more important and pressing aspects to spend your time on.

Selecting a Theme

Theme selection can be fun and exciting; however, it can turn into an overwhelming experience without the right guidance. When selecting a theme, keep the following tips in mind to ensure you select a suitable theme:

Avoid a Header Image

On many business websites there's a huge image that serves to establish the brand and welcome visitors. This image is very important because it's the first thing visitors see. When people select themes with header images, they tend to spend a lot of time searching for a high-resolution image to use and worrying whether it's the right image, and that can be problematic. The time spent looking for a suitable image to use would be better spent on creating content.

Avoid Unnecessary Banner or Homepage Widgets

Many company websites have sections of text that detail what they do and what they're about; although these elements, or widgets, look really cool, they're difficult to set up. These widgets vary a lot across different themes and don't add anything to your content at this point. It's wise to avoid themes with these widgets and focus on things that matter.

Find a Homepage That Can Display Recent Posts Well

The Recent Posts widget is the only widget that should be included on your homepage. This widget displays all your recent posts and automatically updates whenever you publish a new one. Although WordPress offers this widget by default, some themes don't display it prominently on the homepage. Recent posts should be easy to find on your homepage.

Aim for a Simple Set Up

It's tempting to choose a stunning theme with all the bells and whistles. Themes like that typically come with complicated set ups that you want to avoid. The sooner you get set up, the sooner you can start creating high-quality content that will generate traffic.

How to Install and Activate a WordPress Theme

Now that you know what to look for in a WordPress theme, let's go through installing one on your WordPress site.

Note: This process is also covered, step-by-step, in the video version of this training. Purchase access today at **https://stoppingscams.com/FIMP/**.

First, click on the "Appearance" menu option on the left-hand side of your WordPress Dashboard, then click "Themes." This action will navigate to the "Themes" page where you can install and activate themes (see Fig. 04-49).

To add a theme to your WordPress site, click "Add New" to access the "Add Themes" page. This is where all the available themes can be previewed, selected, and installed on your site.

Going through all the available themes will take hours, if not days. Take my advice and select a theme that has no image header and is clean, easy

Fig. 04-49
WordPress Dashboard, Appearance, "Themes" page. Note
that when hovering over a theme, additional options such
as Theme Details, Activate, and Live Preview are displayed.

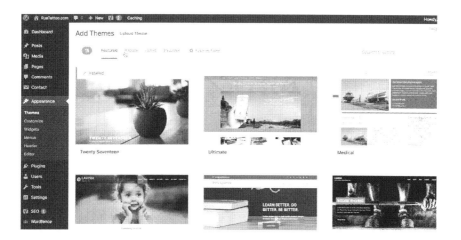

Fig. 04-50
WordPress Dashboard, Appearance, Themes,
"Add Themes" page.

to navigate, and mobile-responsive. Also keep in
mind that like plugins, it's better to choose one
that's regularly updated for security purposes.

How to Check If A Theme Is Mobile-Responsive

A mobile-responsive website adjusts accordingly to the screen from which it's viewed, which in most cases these days is a mobile device. A site should be mobile-responsive because mobile use is on the rise and you want to reach as many people as possible. When visitors encounter your site on a mobile phone and find that it's not mobile-responsive, they will more than likely click away.

Being mobile-responsive also benefits your site in terms of SEO. Google has recently announced that mobile friendly sites will essentially be favored when it comes to ranking.

So, how do you check if the theme you like is mobile-responsive?

The easiest way to check is by resizing the browser you're using to examine the theme (make sure it's not maximized before doing this). Simply drag the corner of the browser window until it's resized to tablet or mobile phone proportions. If the layout changes based on the window size, that is, the page elements rearrange so that you don't need to scroll horizontally, that means it's responsive.

Another way to check mobile responsiveness is on a mobile phone. If your chosen theme has a dedicated demo site, type the URL into a browser on your mobile phone. If the elements are rearranged, the theme is responsive.

 If you're *still* not sure, use Google's Mobile-Friendly Test page (*https://search.google.com/test/mobile-friendly*). It's fairly easy to use: enter the URL of the demo site then click "Run Test." Google will notify if the theme is mobile-responsive or not.

4.11 Creating Your Site's "Core Content" and Menu

Now that the basic structure and design of your website is complete, it's time to start creating core content and building a navigation menu.

Core content refers to content that every website should have, which includes an About page, a Contact page, a Privacy Policy page, and a Terms and Conditions page.

The About Page

People tend to get stuck here as well because they believe the About page needs to be very specific. However, what the About page should accomplish is allow your visitors to connect with you and your website in a personal way. Thus, **the About page can be about pretty much anything:** it can be anything about you, your niche, your passion, or your journey.

Ideally, **it'll tie you into the brand you're building.** You can do that by discussing your experience, especially if you've worked in the industry for many years, and your certifications, if you have any. Or, if your experience is lacking yet you consider it a passion, discuss how much you enjoy it. There are no specific requirements when it comes to what you should write about for the About page. Don't overthink it; write what comes to mind and tweak it afterwards.

Limit the content to three to five paragraphs. People don't want to read a dissertation; they just want a brief introduction to you and your website.

I would also highly recommend adding an image. If you want to use your own image but are worried about privacy, you can do what I do: publish your first name and *never* your full last name. You have the option to pick an alias or pen name, but that may get confusing if you end up creating many sites and using different pen names for each one.

If you're uncomfortable publishing your own photo and want to keep things private, use a stock image instead. A great place to find nice stock images is *Pixabay.com*.

The Contact Page

A Contact page in its simplest form should contain a friendly invitation for visitors to reach out and contact you as well as a contact form with name and email fields, a brief subject line to describe the topic of their message, and the actual message. You can also add a disclaimer that you're asking for an email address ONLY so that you can reply to their message.

The Privacy Policy and Terms and Conditions Pages

First, a very firm disclosure: **I am in NO WAY qualified to give legal advice.** Consult an attorney for very important, high-stakes situations.

That said, based on discussions with attorneys over the years, my understanding is that legal writing is not copyrighted. Technically, you can copy any legal document you find online and replace the company name or website URL with *your* company or domain name. Again, I am not a lawyer, so for specific legal disclaimers, it's better to consult an actual attorney.

There are also a number of free generators online for privacy policies and terms and conditions. One thing to remember when using a free generator is that you need to select the option in Yoast to not index these pages because it's duplicate content. This is similar to what is outlined in Section 4.9 of this chapter (indicating specific pages not to be indexed by search engines).

Setting Up the About Page

VERY Important Note: Shortly before we published this book, Wordpress **dramatically** redesigned their visual page and post editor, so your screens won't quite match up with those in this book by default.

You can switch back to Wordpress' "classic editor" very easily, which will make all of your screens when drafting pages or posts on your website match up with those within this book.

Just search the internet using a phrase along the lines of "**how to change back to Wordpress classic editor**" and you should be able to find multiple articles and videos that will walk you through this process step-by-step in less than five minutes.

First, to add a page, you need to go to your WordPress Dashboard and click on "Pages" on the left-hand side of the page. Then click "Add New."

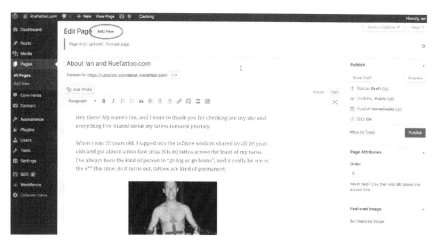

Fig. 04-51

WordPress Dashboard, Pages, Add New, Edit Page. Note
that Edit Page is now displayed because a new page was
already added and saved as a draft.

When creating your About page, it's advisable to
optimize it for your domain name. For example, I
optimized my About page using "RueTattoo.com"
as my focus keyword so that when someone
searches "Rue Tattoo" or "RueTattoo.com," my
page is likely to come up in the search results.
Yoast SEO assists with this, so we'll cover on-page
SEO extensively in a later chapter. For now, suf-
fice it to say that we want search engines to index
your About page. Since I want to optimize for
"RueTattoo.com," I've placed that keyword in the
page title, the permalink, the meta description,
and as an attribute in the image I included.

Setting Up the Contact Page

Similar to the About Page, go to your WordPress Dashboard and click on "Pages" on the left-hand side of the page, and then click "Add New."

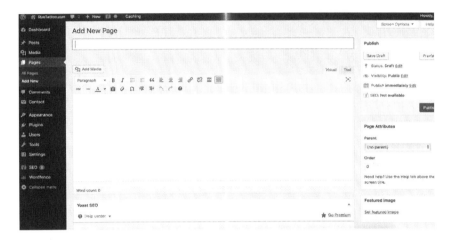

Fig. 04-52
WordPress Dashboard, Pages, Add New, Add New Page.

The Contact page should contain a friendly invitation from you to your visitors to reach out. For example, here's what my Contact page says:

"Looking for something you can't find on our website, for some personal advice from someone that's 'been there,' or just wanting to say 'thanks' for something you saw here on RueTattoo.com? Just fill out the form below and I'll send you a reply as soon as I can!"

That's only the invitation. To include the actual form, go back to the Contact Form 7 plugin you installed, copy the shortcode for the form, and then paste it into the page.

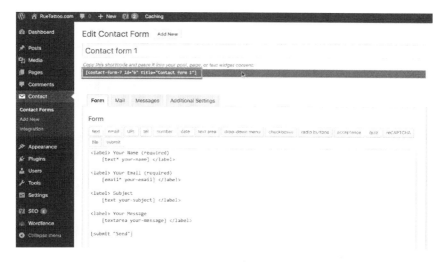

Fig. 04-53
WordPress Dashboard, Contact, Contact Forms, Edit
Contact Form. Note the shortcode highlighted in blue.

Once you publish the Contact page with the pasted
shortcode, here's what the page will look like:

Contact

Looking for something you can't find on the website, for some personal
advice from someone that's "been there", or just wanting to say "thanks"
for something you saw here on RueTattoo.com? Just fill out the form below and I'll send you a reply as soon as I can!

Your Name (required)

Your Email (required)

Subject

Your Message

SEND

Fig. 04-54
RueTattoo.com Contact Page.

Everything that was set up in Section 4.9 when you installed Contact Form 7 is now ready. As soon as someone fills out the form and clicks "Send," all the information will be sent to ian@ruetattoo.com.

Even if your Contact page is basic, it's good practice to optimize it. Doing so won't hurt anything, and it's a personal preference of mine. Yoast SEO saves the day again with this process. Scroll down to the bottom of the Contact page until you find the Yoast SEO section.

Fig. 04-55
WordPress Dashboard, Pages, All Pages, Edit Page,
Contact Page, scrolled down to 'Yoast SEO" section. Pay
attention to the SEO title, Slug, and Meta description.

The "SEO title" is the title that's displayed in search results. The "slug" is the part of the URL that comes after your domain name. In this example, the slug is "contact," which makes the complete URL of the page: *https://ruetattoo.com/contact/*. The "meta description" isn't strictly for SEO purposes, but more to compel visitors viewing the search results to click on your link.

I didn't set a focus keyword here because I'm not really trying to rank for anything except my brand name. Clicking "Publish" makes the page available to everyone.

Setting Up the Privacy Policy and Terms and Conditions Pages

 You can find Privacy Policy and Terms of Service generators through a quick Google search, but a particular generator found on *BenNadel.com* is very useful. Entering the company name (yourcompanyname.com) and state will display a preview of the generated website terms and conditions.

The nifty thing about this particular generator is that it also generates the terms and conditions in HTML format, meaning you don't have to format the headings and titles; all you need to do is copy and paste the HTML code into the text editor of the intended WordPress page and it's ready to go. Here's what I mean:

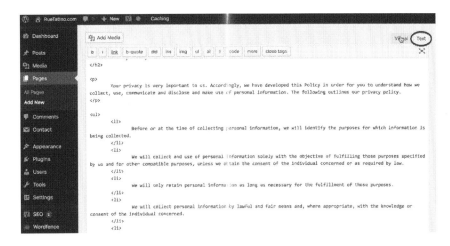

Fig. 04-56
WordPress Dashboard, Pages, Add New, Add New Page.
Note that the "Text" tab is selected instead of the "Visual"
tab for editing in the upper right-hand of the page.

Note that I'm combining the Terms and Conditions and Privacy Policy in one page. I'm also going to optimize the page through Yoast SEO:

- SEO title = "RueTattoo.com Terms, Conditions, and Privacy Policy"

- Slug = "terms-conditions-privacy-policy"

- Meta description = "RueTattoo.com website terms and conditions as well as our privacy policy, can be found here."

Because we used a generator for the content of this page, it's likely the same content is found on Terms and Conditions pages of other websites. It's important to tell search engines not to index this page to avoid our search engine rankings going down because Google thinks we have duplicate content.

The way to do this is also through Yoast SEO: click on the gear icon on the left-hand side of the Yoast SEO section of the page to go to the "Advanced settings." Then, set the "Meta robots index" to "noindex" and click "Publish" to publish the page (see Fig. 04-57).

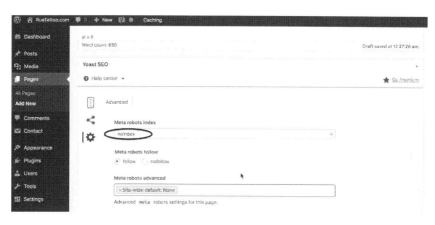

Fig. 04-57
WordPress Dashboard, Pages, Add New, Edit Page, Terms and Conditions Page, scrolled down to "Yoast SEO" section, "Advanced settings" tab. Note the "Meta robots index" dropdown menu is set to "noindex."

Setting Up the Navigation Menu

The last step of this process is to set up a navigation menu that displays the pages that were just set up.

Find and click on the menu option titled "Appearance" on the left-hand side of the WordPress Dashboard. Then, click on "Menus" to pull up the "Edit Menus" page. Enter a name for your menu (I titled my menu "Main Menu") and then click "Create Menu" on the right.

Fig. 04-58
*WordPress Dashboard, Appearance, Menus, Edit Menus.
Note the "Menu Name" field and "Create Menu" button
to the right. Also note that the pages we just set up are
displayed on the left.*

Next, select all the pages you just created and click "Add to Menu."

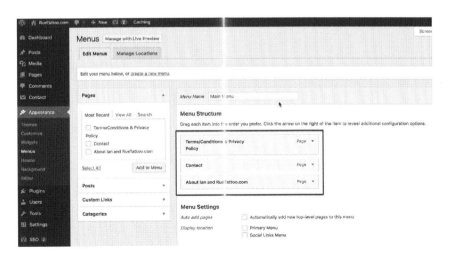

Fig. 04-59
*WordPress Dashboard, Appearance, Menus, Edit Menus
with pages added to the menu.*

Notice that the pages you selected now appear under "Menu Structure" (see Fig. 04-59). Next, add a link to the homepage by clicking "Custom Links," entering the homepage URL and the name to display, and then clicking "Add to Menu" (see Fig. 04-60).

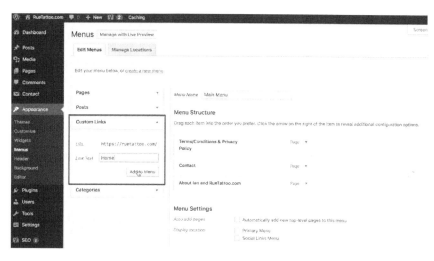

Fig. 04-60

WordPress Dashboard, Appearance, Menus, Edit Menus with pages added to the menu and "Custom Link" fields being filled out. Clicking "Add to Menu" will add it to the "Menu Structure" section.

The pages under "Menu Structure" can be reorganized by dragging them, and whatever order they're set in is the order they'll appear in the menu. The best order to set your pages is Home page first, About page second, and the Contact page third. Also, the Terms and Conditions & Privacy Policy should be a dropdown underneath the About page. That way, if someone hovers over the "About" menu option they will see the Terms and Conditions & Privacy Policy page.

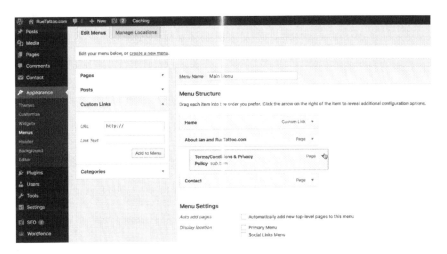

Fig. 04-61
*WordPress Dashboard, Appearance, Menus, Edit Menus with pages
and "Custom Link" added to the menu (in the desired order). Note that
the "Terms and Conditions & Privacy Policy" page is added as a sub-
option under the "About" page. Also note the "Menu Settings" section
below the "Menu Structure" section.*

Checking "Automatically add new top-level pages
option" means every time you create a new page,
it will automatically be added to your menu, and
you don't normally want that automated. What
you DO need to check is the "Primary Menu"
option. If you miss checking this option, your navigation menu won't be visible to visitors.

If you want to have links open in new tabs, you
can do that by tweaking some settings in your
Dashboard. First, click on the "Screen Options"
pull tab at the top of the page to expand it. Then,
you need to select "Link Target" (see Fig. 04-62).

Once "Link Target" is selected, an option will
appear under "Menu Structure" to open the link in
a new tab (see Fig. 04-63).

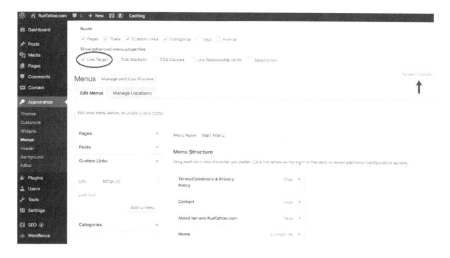

Fig. 04-62

WordPress Dashboard, Appearance, Menus, Edit Menus, with "Screen Options" expanded and "Link Target" selected.

Fig. 04-63

WordPress Dashboard, Appearance, Menus, Edit Menus, with "Open link in a new tab" option shown under "Terms/Conditions & Privacy Policy" page.

Selecting the "Open link in a new tab" option for a page will open it in a new tab when it's clicked in the menu. For your website pages, it doesn't matter if they open in a new tab. However, for external links, such as affiliate links or links to your social media accounts, it's best to have them open in a new tab so people don't navigate away from your website unnecessarily.

Once you're done with set up, click "Save Menu." It's then good practice to go to the website and check if the navigation menu is displaying properly.

4.12 Setting Up Google Analytics & Google Search Console for Helpful Data

It's important to put foundations in place to receive analytics and data for your website. Even if you're not seeing traffic right now, setting up Google Analytics and Google Search Console will show you when your site starts receiving traffic and seeing traction. Although not needed for a while, you're going to be happy you set them up early when that time comes.

Note: If watching this in action is more helpful, you can purchase access to the step-by-step video version of this training at **https://stoppingscams.com/FIMP/**.

Setting Up Google Analytics

Google Analytics is a free service offered by Google that tracks website traffic and gives insight into how users find, use, and interact with websites.

First, navigate to the Google Analytics homepage. If you don't already have a Google or Gmail account that you want to associate with your website, you'll need to create one. To do so, select "More options" and then click "Create account."

 Tip: It's wise to create a separate Google account to use only for the purposes of your website. Having separate personal and business Google accounts will save time and grief in the long run.

Fig. 04-64
Google Analytics homepage displaying the Google sign in
form with "More options" already clicked and displaying
the "Create account" option.

When you're done creating a Google account, go back to the Google Analytics homepage and click "Sign up."

Fig. 04-65

Google Analytics homepage displaying "Sign up" button on the right.

Clicking the "Sign up" button will navigate you to a form asking for information about your website.

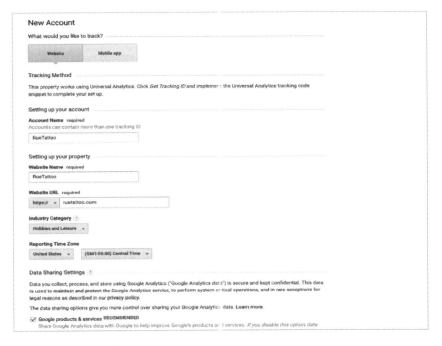

Fig. 04-66

Google Analytics "sign up" page with fields filled out.

Once you've filled out all the fields, click "Get Tracking ID." You'll be prompted to accept the website terms in order to receive a Tracking ID and Tracking Code.

Fig. 04-67
Google Analytics homepage with Tracking ID displayed
and Website Tracking code selected.

Your Tracking ID identifies your Google Analytics account. This is included in your tracking code, a code that needs to be added to your website to allow Google Analytics to gather data.

First, you'll need to install a plugin for headers and footers. Go back to your WordPress Dashboard, click "Plugins" then "Add New." Then, search for "header and footer" and install the plugin titled "Insert Headers and Footers."

Fig. 04-68
WordPress Dashboard, Plugins, Add New, search "header and footer," install "Insert Headers and Footers" plugin.

Once you've activated the Insert Headers and Footers plugin, you can access it by clicking "Settings" on the left-hand side of the page, then clicking "Insert Headers and Footers." Now copy the tracking code from Google Analytics and paste it under "Scripts in Header" in WordPress and click "Save."

Fig. 04-69

WordPress Dashboard, Settings, Insert Headers and Footers, "Settings" page, "Scripts in Header" text box containing tracking code.

After successfully saving the tracking code in the header script, Google Analytics will track all the pages on your website, compile and analyze the data in your Google Analytics account, and allow you to access the information when logged in to Google Analytics. Note that it may take a couple of hours for Google Analytics to receive data. If it's been days and you're sure you've been receiving traffic, yet Google Analytics isn't reflecting that, contact Google Analytics customer support.

Setting Up Google Search Console

Google Search Console is another free Google service that monitors a website's presence in Google Search results. It's not strictly required to sign up for this service, however, it can really help optimize your website's performance in search results by providing information on how Google views your website.

First, go to the Google Search Console homepage and log in using your Google username and password. Logging in will take you to a welcome page where you can add your website.

Fig. 04-70
Google Search Console "Welcome" page with website input.

An important thing to remember here is that when entering your website, enter it EXACTLY as it is shown in your WordPress settings. To verify the exact address of your website, go to your WordPress Dashboard, click on "Settings" on the left-hand side of the page, then find the "Site Address (URL)" field. The URL in that field needs to exactly match the one you submit to Google Search Console. Otherwise it won't work.

Fig. 04-71
WordPress Dashboard, Settings, "General Settings" page.
Note the "Site Address (URL)" field.

After double-checking your site address (URL) in WordPress, go back to Google Search Console and enter your website URL. Then, click "Add A Property."

Things are going to get a little tricky here, so please bear with me.

Clicking "Add A Property" will navigate to a page where you're asked to verify the ownership of your website. Click on "Alternate Methods" and then "HTML tag."

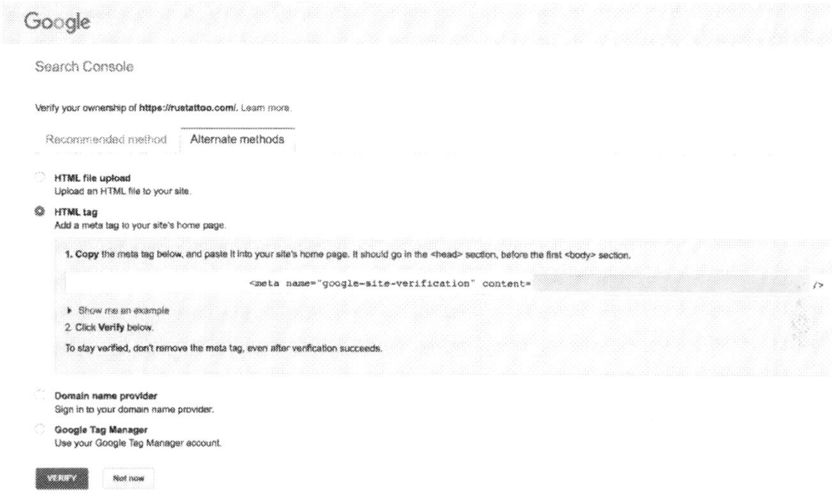

Fig. 04-72
Google Search Console, Verify Ownership, "Alternate methods" tab selected, "HTML tag" selected.

Copy the Meta Tag generated and go back to your WordPress Dashboard. Click "SEO" on the left-hand side of the page to go to the Yoast SEO settings. Click the "Webmaster tools" tab, look for the field that says "Google Search Console," paste the Meta Tag copied from Google Search Console, and click "Save changes."

Fig. 04-73
WordPress Dashboard, Yoast SEO Dashboard, "Webmaster tools" tab. Note the "Google Search Console" text field.

Once changes have been saved in Yoast, go back to Google Search Console and click "Verify." If the steps were completed correctly, Google Search Console will display a confirmation message that looks like this:

Fig. 04-74
Google Search Console, Confirmation message that ownership has been verified.

Now it's official: **you've completely set up your website!**

Your newly-created website is now ready to be filled with quality content. In Chapter 5 I'm going to outline everything you need to know about keyword research.

Chapter 4 Summary

|||||||||||||||||||||||||||||||||||||||||||||||||||||||||||||||||||||||||||||||||||||||||||||||||||

- There's absolutely no way you can build a stable and profitable internet business without your own website.

- Establish an independent mindset now. You need to have a self-seeking, independent mentality to be able to successfully create your website and online business.

- You don't need an exact match domain; in fact, it might even harm your website.

- Your domain name should meet the following criteria (in order of priority):

    o Have a ".com" domain suffix

    o Be memorable, brandable, and easy to spell

    o be as short as possible (3 words maximum)

    o No hyphens or numbers

    o Include a root keyword

- If you've done everything to go with .com but can't find an acceptable domain name, consider only ".net" or ".org."

- There is no 100% perfect domain name. You'll have to make some compromises but having these guidelines in mind will help you select a domain name that's close to it.

- Some useful tools to get ideas for domain names include Lean Domain Search, NameMesh.com, and NameBoy.

- There are three major options to register your domain name: through the hosting company, GoDaddy.com, or Namecheap.com.

- Namecheap offers the best value for money in the long term and is therefore my top recommendation for registering your domain name.

- Start with shared hosting first and aim to eventually outgrow that into dedicated servers.

- Bluehost offers the best service and support over any other low-cost shared hosting company I've worked with and is therefore my top recommendation for hosting.

- Sign up for unlimited domains up front because you're likely to need that down the road.

- If you registered your domain separately from your hosting provider, you'll need to update your nameservers on your domain registrar. For instructions, consult the websites of your domain registrar and hosting provider.

- WordPress is the best CMS to use because of its customization, wide customer and knowledge base, and superior plugin collection.

- Once you've set up WordPress, delete the default post and pages to avoid confusion.

- If you set up WordPress through Bluehost, you can delete the following plugins: Akismet, Hello Dolly, Jetpack, MOJO Marketplace, Optin Monster, WPForms Lite.

- Install the following recommended plugins instead: Yoast SEO for SEO, Easy Updates Manager for handling updates for WordPress, plugins, and themes, Wordfence for security, and Contact Form 7 for contact forms.

- Adjusting your site's permalink structure to the post name is essential for SEO.

- Changing your display name from your username to your nickname is crucial for security purposes.

- When selecting plugins, select those that are highly ranked and regularly updated.

- When starting out, the only things that matter in terms of website design are that your website is clean, easy to navigate, and mobile responsive.

- Your website's core content includes your About Page, Contact Page, a Privacy Policy page, and a Terms and Conditions page.

- Set up your navigation menu early on so that visitors can easily navigate through the pages of your site.

- If you plan to include links to other sites in your navigation menu, it's best to have them open in new tabs so your visitors don't navigate away from your website unnecessarily.

- It's really important to set up Google Analytics and Google Search Console as early as possible so that you can get really good analytics and data on your website.

- Google Analytics and Google Search Console are both free services; the only requirement is a Google account.

Chapter 5: "The Frame" — Lethal Keyword Research

Keyword research is either going to be your best friend or your worst enemy. It'll help your internet business thrive or kill it before it ever gets off the ground.

In this chapter, I'll share actionable, step-by-step strategies for picking high-profit keywords that WILL result in traffic, even in the most competitive niches.

5.1 How Keyword Research Will Make or Break Your Entire Business

Keyword research is fundamental to success in Internet and Affiliate Marketing, and even more so in any aspect of an online business that's dependent on SEO, such as blogging, content creation, and content marketing. In this section of Chapter 5, I'm going to discuss why keyword research is such a crucial determiner of success in an internet business.

What Is a Keyword?

A **keyword** is a word or phrase used in search engines when a person is seeking information. For the sake of simplicity, I'll refer to both search words and phrases as keywords. For example, if someone wants to learn about tattoo removal, they may type "what is tattoo removal?" in a Google Search. That question is a keyword.

To have a successful internet business, you need a website. Think of your website as the foundation of your internet business, while the keywords you choose to write content about make up the frame.

Why You Should Bother with Keywords

In a nutshell, you want your content to be found by the right people. Pay attention to what your target audience will likely type into their search engines so you can take that into consideration when creating content. Ideally, your content will be in their search results pages.

Unfortunately, keyword research is commonly overlooked in Internet Marketing training materials. The following example should illustrate just how crucial keyword research is to your business.

A Tale of Two Brothers

Once there were two brothers who each built niche sites. The first brother didn't follow the FIMP niche selection training, yet still managed to select a decent niche. Though far from the perfect niche, it was sufficient. He purchased and registered the first domain name that came to mind without regard to keywords, and although his content is far from the best of the best, it's certainly above average. He doesn't have any social media presence.

BUT, he selects keywords very diligently and takes the time to research them before creating slightly above average content for his okay niche. On top of that, he executes on-page SEO perfectly.

The second brother follows all of the training at FIMP, ticks all the checkboxes outlined, and selects an *incredible* niche. He comes up with a clever brand and domain that's short and easy to remember. He writes incredibly high-quality content, some of the best content on the web, and leverages his social media.

BUT, he doesn't select his keywords very strategically and writes about topics without doing any keyword research. He creates content that *HE* believes will be searched by his audience.

While the first brother disregarded a fair amount of what FIMP teaches and selected an okay niche,

5.1 HOW KEYWORD RESEARCH WILL MAKE OR BREAK YOUR ENTIRE BUSINESS

by contrast, the second brother followed the training perfectly but focused on writing content and not getting tied up in all the details of keyword research.

If I asked you who, between the two brothers, will end up more successful, you might select the second brother. After all, he did select a better niche, formulated a clever brand, spent more time on social media, and wrote higher quality content.

However, the first brother has a much better shot at success than the second one. Even though his niche is "just okay," his domain name isn't too clever, and his promotional efforts are nonexistent, the fact that he does keyword research diligently and optimizes his content around the keywords that he selects makes a huge difference.

What We Learn from the Two Brothers

 Poorly chosen or completely ignored keyword research is going to equal inefficient SEO. If search engines aren't finding your content, then you're going to get fewer, or possibly zero, traffic. As discussed, traffic equals money. If you're receiving no traffic, you're going to earn no money. That's how keyword research ties directly to your bottom line and how much revenue your website is going to generate.

Wait... What About Niche Selection?

I know - I harped on and on about niche selection being crucial to your Internet Marketing success. The truth is, **niche selection without keyword research will amount to nothing.** Picking the right niche is a crucial first step; next to that is keyword research.

When it comes to building a profitable internet business, your efforts will be cumulative. You want to get the essential steps right during the early stages because the more you stack onto an unstable foundation, the more likely everything will tumble and collapse.

Keyword Research: What to Expect

Keep in mind that while niche selection appears to be subjective and more of an art form, keyword research is much more data-driven and scientific. There are solid criteria when deciding whether a keyword is a good, or not-so-good, option.

5.1 HOW KEYWORD RESEARCH WILL MAKE OR BREAK YOUR ENTIRE BUSINESS

5.2 The Anatomy of the "Perfect" Keyword

|||||||||||||||||||||||||||||||||||||||||||||||||||||||||||||||||||||||||||||||||||||||||||||||||||

Traditional Keyword Selection

For years, Internet Marketers have chased keywords that are the perfect combination of **high search volume and low competition.** Basically, they chased unicorns.

High search volume keywords are searched as much as possible every month. Low competition keywords are generally those that have little to no content ranking for it. When you target low competition keywords, your chances of ranking at the top of search results, or at least the first page, are higher.

Why Traditional Doesn't Cut It Anymore

Today's internet is more competitive than ever, with the total number of active websites in the hundreds of millions. It has become more and more difficult to find high search volume keywords that would be easy to rank for.

As a result of the internet's continuous evolution, Internet Marketing changes very rapidly. Every two or three years things get turned upside down and revolutionized. Google periodically changes their search engine algorithm so websites that use shady techniques to rank high on search result pages are penalized and websites that have high-quality content (i.e., more useful for Google's users) are ranked higher.

Of course, all algorithms have their weaknesses. With a little technical know-how, you can beat Google at their own game. Trying this strategy is a terribly difficult way of ranking your website, though. Google is aware that people try to find ways around their algorithms and actively work to block and circumvent them. You'll be much better off and waste less time playing by Google's rules and creating high-quality content rather than trying to game the system.

Because of (or maybe in spite of) the internet's rapid changes, higher search volume keywords are usually dominated by high-authority established websites. These websites have been around for a long time and have hundreds, if not thousands, of pages of high-quality content. The reason these sites devote resources to creating content that targets higher search volume keywords is to rank for those keywords and get more traffic, creating more opportunities to make money.

Those who are just starting out in Internet Marketing have very little chance to compete with these big websites in terms of resources and content. So, what's a beginner to do?

Flip the Script: Scraps Today, Feasts Tomorrow

Instead of searching for high search volume and low competition keywords, build up your site by picking up the scraps that all of the big boys are leaving behind. Most of these authority sites want nothing to do with a keyword that has 30, 100, or 500 searches a month. Why would they if they can target keywords that have a thousand or more searches a month?

Build on the scraps the giants are leaving behind. These keywords may have 15, 30, 45, or 100 searches a month, but, in time, your website's authority will build on those little scraps and you'll eventually be able to compete with high-authority sites. It takes at least 6 to 12 months to get there, but you may start seeing traction before then, even with lower search volume keywords.

Turning out high-quality content that directly targets lower search volume keywords that are being overlooked adds up over time. Instead of spending the next eight months trying to rank a single keyword that gets 5,000 searches a month, spend those months focusing on dozens of keywords that have 30 to 100 searches a month. In today's search climate you'll have a better shot at getting ranked for many of those lower search volume keywords than getting ranked for one high search volume keyword in the same amount of time.

People are going to start noticing you as your content gets ranked for lower search volume keyword articles and you build your website's authority. They will link to your content and talk about you in various forums. The more your site gets talked about, the more credibility and authority your site gains, and you can eventually use this authority to rank for moderate-to-high competition keywords.

This process will take some time to get to the point where your site is seeing success. Once it gets to that tipping point, tremendous growth follows, which is a sign of gaining authority. What you've written prior to this tipping point also begins to rank in search engine results because your authority is building.

This is why for early-stage blogs, especially those that don't have a large marketing budget, frequent publishing of high-quality content is common. This is why only aiming for desirable search terms that have a few thousand searches each month is going to result in disappointment. And this is why you should steer clear of Internet Marketers who tell you otherwise.

5.3 How to Use Keywords to Ignite Your Content

IIIIIIIIIIIIIIIIIIIIIIIIIIIIIIIIIIIIIIIIIIIIIIIIIIIIIIIIIIIIIIIIIIIIIIIIIIIIIIIIIIIIIIIIIIIIIIIIIIIIIIII

Now that you know *what* type of keyword works, you can now learn *how* to use keywords to grow your internet business.

Using Keywords to Write Quality Content

The first step is to find one or two keywords you want to target in an article. Some people target three to five keywords; you can try to do that, too, but you're going to spread yourself so thin that you might as well have not tried to optimize for any keyword. Personally, I pick and write about a single keyword.

Writing high-quality content around a single keyword results in articles ranking for other related keywords around the topic. Search engines are now enhancing their algorithms so that contextually related keywords in the content are considered. Writing high-quality content increases the likelihood that people will share and link to your article. Search engines also look at the quality of websites that link back to your content when they consider how to rank your article.

Once you've decided the keyword you want to target, **write a high-quality post around that**

keyword and aim for it to be better than anything else on the internet.

It sounds ambitious, but that should always be the driving force behind your writing. If you're very familiar with the topic, then it's time to show it. If you know the topic well enough but not enough to write "the best article ever," then it's time to do some research. Your goal should always be to create content that is more helpful than what anybody else has written. Aiming for anything less won't do your business any favors.

High-quality posts don't have to be very long. It's possible to have excellent content that contains 1,200 to 1,500 words. All your articles need not be 5,000 words long. However, remember to be realistic: 300 to 500-word articles are likely not going to be the best quality posts on any topic. To be truly helpful, your content needs be detailed and discuss the topic extensively. That's not possible with a 500-word article.

After you've written your post, you can then **optimize it for your target keyword.** This involves SEO, which I'll discuss in more detail in a later chapter. Basically, we want Google and other search engines to notice your high-quality content, so we work to get them to do just that. SEO involves tweaking certain elements of a post, and it's a bit too complicated to get into at this time. Just keep in mind that this is the next step after creating a post.

So, You've Published a Keyword-Optimized Post - Now What?

Now we wait.

In time, your website will build authority and start ranking for the terms you're targeting. Building authority and search engine rankings doesn't happen overnight. It's possible to dedicate six to eight months finding keywords to write and publish great content for. Meanwhile, nothing's happening to your traffic and you wonder if you're doing everything correctly.

If you find yourself in this position and consider giving up, reread Chapter 2 and review the Mindset Training. It's normal to get stuck in a rut at some points of your Internet Marketing journey. Internet Marketing is a challenging endeavor, just like any other business. Keep finding keywords and writing and optimizing posts and the results you've been aiming for will come.

Once that happens, new content will rank (including older posts). As your entire site's authority builds, a lot of your content that formerly didn't have enough authority will start to rank higher. Sometimes, especially when it's high-quality, your content will rank for keywords you didn't even target or optimize.

 Optimizing content for the right keywords brings in more traffic, which eventually brings in more money. Don't lose sight of that.

What to Look for in a Keyword

I've talked extensively about finding keywords, but what *characteristics* should you specifically look for in a keyword?

At least 30 to 100 Searches a Month: anything less and you'll need to write more content for more keywords. Anything more and you'll have difficulty ranking those keywords. Keywords that have 30 to 100 searches a month hit a balance between the effort required to write content and the difficulty of ranking in search engines.

Lower Competition Keywords Are Preferable: exactly how to determine if a keyword is low-competition is a combination of different factors that I'll discuss more in depth in a later chapter.

You *can* do keyword research every time you write a new article, but I prefer to do keyword research in chunks that will last at least a few weeks, or about six to 10 articles. When I run out of keywords, I go back and do another chunk of keyword research.

I've found that this is the most efficient way of conducting keyword research. Rather than spending several hours focusing on finding a single keyword, writing the article, then repeating the entire process again, I've found that it's better to do keyword research in one go and focus time on writing the next several articles over the next few weeks.

5.4 Qualified Traffic vs. Unqualified Traffic

The next step is to gauge whether a keyword is valuable for the niche you're writing for. Why are some keywords in your niche valuable while others are totally worthless? This comes down to whether the keywords you're selecting are attracting qualified versus unqualified traffic.

What Makes Traffic Qualified?

Simply put, qualified traffic is traffic from visitors who are likely to take action on your website. These visitors are likely to subscribe to your mailing list or buy from you or your affiliates. What makes them qualified is that they are actively searching for what you have to offer. This is why it's important to take their intent into consideration when selecting keywords.

Not All Traffic Is Created Equal

Just because a keyword in your niche has high search volume and low competition doesn't necessarily mean that it's viable. If the visitors that your keywords attract aren't likely to take action on your website, they're worthless. It doesn't matter if they're interested in reading your content or if there are 10,000 of them a month; if visitors don't take action on your site, they are useless. **Unqualified traffic is worthless traffic.**

This is what it all boils down to: not all traffic is created equal.

I wish someone had explained the concept of qualified traffic to me when I started out. This mistake is more commonly made by new Internet Marketers, but I've also seen it done by people who are five-figure monthly earners. Even now, I see plenty of very successful advanced Internet Marketers who aren't paying attention to this concept. They go after ALL the traffic they can without even considering whether or not it's going to result in anything that's beneficial.

If you're unfamiliar with this concept going into Internet Marketing, it can really bite you in the butt. Getting 30,000 visitors a month in unqualified traffic won't get you more than $1,000 a month no matter how much you optimize for conversions or what offers you promote.

My Story: An Example of How Unqualified Traffic Can Hurt Return on Investment

 StoppingScams.com is where I provide honest Internet Marketing and Affiliate Marketing product reviews. When *StoppingScams.com* was fairly new I was trying to build authority. I wanted to transition from doing reviews to something more holistic, so I decided to write an article about how a Multi-Level Marketing (MLM) company ruined one of my friendships.

I had a friend who tried to recruit me into an MLM company called *Nerium* that sells anti-aging skincare and wellness products. The experience destroyed our friendship, and I wrote about it both as an honest review and as a cautionary tale about success in MLMs.

If you're interested, you can read the article, titled How MLMs Ruin Friendships – My 100% Honest Nerium Review, *on https://stoppingscams.com/.*

Since then, I've received thousands of visitors for this article because it ranks well for terms like "Nerium scam" and other long-tail keywords related to *Nerium*. Of course, when you receive that kind of traffic, you want to try and convert it. And try I did. However, no matter what conversion optimization technique I did (and I know plenty), that traffic just would not convert for Internet Marketing training or how to build an online business.

To this day, I still receive over a hundred or more visitors a day from this article. But I don't get anything out of it because **they just don't convert into my particular funnel.**

You would think someone interested in knowing about an MLM opportunity is also interested in building an Affiliate Marketing business or blog, but they're not. They're only interested in that specific MLM opportunity, not making money online.

I'm not alone in this. Other marketers who compete in the same space as *StoppingScams.com* write a lot about MLMs and see a ton of traffic. However, they don't see a whole lot of conversion into Internet Marketing training because there just isn't an overlap between visitors who are interested in both extra and passive income.

So that's my very real, very painful example of unqualified traffic that doesn't convert.

The moral of the story is clear: just because there are keywords with search volume that you could potentially get rankings for doesn't mean it's worth your time or that it's going to make you money.

How to Avoid Unqualified Traffic

When looking at high search volume keywords, consider first if that keyword is actually related to what you're promoting. Your new content should relate closely enough to your existing content, as well as the offers you're promoting, so you can convert the traffic you *do* receive.

Between a higher search volume keyword that's only loosely related to your existing offers and content and a lower search volume keyword that seems to only have a few people searching for it but is much more related to what you're promoting, go for the latter.

As you're looking at keywords and building your keyword list, think:

"Is the person searching for this keyword in my target audience?"

A lot of the time you can tell whether or not you're attracting the right kind of visitor by the keywords they're searching. As you build your website, pay attention to how well the traffic to certain posts is converting. Take note of which keywords are performing better than others to achieve higher conversion rates and, in return, earn income with qualified traffic.

5.5 Finding Keywords Using Free Keyword Tools

Many people who start in Internet Marketing don't have a budget for paid keyword tools, especially since the best ones now include monthly fees instead of a one-time subscription fee.

Before I dive into how to use free keyword tools, let me first discuss the pros and cons of using them.

Free Keyword Tools: The Pros

An obvious pro of free keyword tools is that there are **no added expenses** after you've paid for your domain name and hosting.

People in this industry claim that your domain name and hosting aren't enough to build a website. To be honest, it's more than enough. The biggest expense in this industry is the training, which you're already getting in this book. The next biggest expense is the hosting and domain name. If you're willing to put in the legwork with free keyword tools, then you've got everything you need to get a profitable internet business started.

This is the only real pro of free keyword tools. For plenty of people, that's more than enough reason to use them. Don't let anyone make you think that quality keywords are impossible to find outside of premium keyword tools. It's more work, for sure, but with the right tools and the right method, you'll be able to find quality keywords.

Free Keyword Tools: The Cons

The not-so-good news about using free keyword tools is that they **don't provide much data on competition.** You'll get some data, but it's not going to be as good as what the premium keyword tools provide. Plus, most free keyword tools don't provide an easy, at-a-glance presentation. This makes research a little bit trickier and a little more overwhelming because you'll have to manually interpret a lot of the data.

Another disadvantage of using free keyword tools is that most of the time, **the data provided is not as accurate or reliable** as the data provided by premium tools (Google's free keyword tool being the exception).

Lastly, using free keyword tools **takes about five to ten times longer than premium tools.** Over time you'll get better and quicker at using free keyword tools, but it's still going to take more time investment.

The Best Free Keyword Tools Available

There are a number of quality free keyword tools available online; you just have to find them. The most reliable of them all is the Google AdWords Keyword Planner, also known as the Google Keyword Planner.

To use this tool, you'll need a Google AdWords account. Let me be clear: *that doesn't mean you need to spend any money with AdWords.* You just need to go through the process of setting up an AdWords account. During set up, you'll be asked questions like:

"What do you want to buy keywords for?"

"How much is your daily budget?"

Don't provide any credit card information or launch the campaign. Otherwise, you'll actually buy ads on Google, which is not what you want to do if you're trying to avoid spending money.

Other helpful tools include *Keyword.io* and *UberSuggest.io*, which provide lists of relevant keyword suggestions when a seed keyword(s) is entered. These tools are not as helpful or reliable as Google Keyword Planner but do have their uses.

You'll also need *MozBar* (found on Moz.com) an SEO toolbar that checks Search Engine Result Pages (SERP) and assesses the competition and website authority of keywords.

MozBar: Important Metrics to Note

Page Authority

Page Authority (PA) is a score that predicts how well a specific webpage will rank on SERPs.

Scores range from one to 100, with higher scores corresponding to a greater ability to rank. This is the most important metric to pay attention to in MozBar.

When you search for a keyword in Google using MozBar, pay attention to the PA value of the webpages on the first page of the search results; they need to be as close to or below 10 as possible for that keyword to qualify as low-competition because you want to compete with sites that have low PA.

Unfortunately, it's become harder to find keywords with competing pages that have PAs as low as 10. The webpages on the first page of Google typically have PAs of 15 to 25. However, there are always weaknesses in those pages that can be exploited to give you a fighting chance of landing on the first page of Google's search results.

Domain Authority

Domain Authority (DA) is a search engine ranking score that predicts how well a website will rank on SERPs. Similar to PA scores, the higher the score, the greater ability to rank.

Whereas PA refers to the *individual* page, DA refers to the entire domain. For example, while

StoppingScams.com's DA score applies to the entire domain, the PA score varies for every page and blog post on the site.

It's important to note that Moz didn't invent Domain and Page Authority. While the company did come up with proprietary algorithms to compute values for each domain and page, the computations may not be totally accurate. However, keep in mind that Moz's algorithms provide a very close approximation. The only company that knows exactly how authoritative domains and pages actually rank is Google, and they're not about to divulge that information.

Search Result Pages: Important Things to Examine

Meta Title and Meta Description

When researching keywords, check if the resulting pages include the exact keyword in the meta title and meta description (to review these concepts, refer back to section 4.9 of Chapter 4). Frankly, you're likely to see DA and PA scores that are scary. Make it habit to look for gaps during your research, such as the exact keyword being in the meta title and description.

Question-and-Answer Sites

Another thing to take note of is whether the search results for the keyword you're researching include pages from question-and-answer sites such as *Yahoo! Answers*, *Stack Exchange*, or *Quora*. If this is the case, then there aren't many pages with high PA that rank for that particular keyword. The question-and-answer sites tend to get pushed into the first page of results because of their DA scores and not because of the PA score of that particular page. This is actually a good sign because you can deliver a more authoritative individual page for that keyword and end up ranking higher than Q&A sites.

Free Blog Platforms

One more thing that bodes well for new keywords is if the first page of the search results has pages from sites hosted by free blog platforms, such as *WordPress.com*, *Blogspot.com*, or *Tumblr.com*. These pages are easy to spot because they'll include the name of the blog platform in the domain name, such as *stoppingscams.wordpress.com* or *stoppingscams.blogspot.com*. Similar to Q&A sites, these webpages are pushed into the first page of results because of their DA score, and not the PA score. If that's the case, you can outrank them by creating an authoritative blog post around that keyword.

Using Free Keyword Tools to Find High-Quality Keywords

Note: You can purchase the step-by-step video version of this training at **https://stoppingscams.com/FIMP/** *if you prefer to see this in action.*

The first thing you want to do is expand on a **seed keyword**, or the root keyword you want to expand on to find long-tail keywords. *Google Keyword Planner, Keyword.io, or Ubersuggest.io* are all acceptable tools for this process. For the purposes of this lesson, I'm going to use Google Keyword Planner.

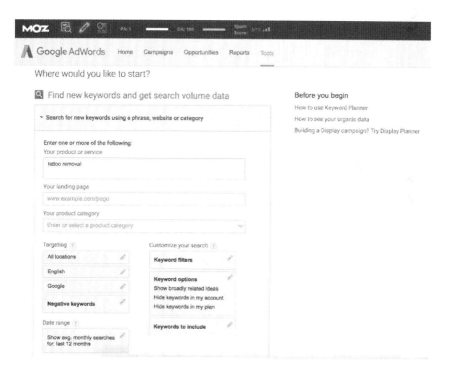

Fig. 05-01

Google Keyword Planner, "Search for new keywords using a phrase, website or category" option selected.

When you've created a Google AdWords account, navigate to the Google Keyword Planner tab and click to expand the dropdown menu titled, "Search for new keywords using a phrase, website or category." Then, enter a seed keyword into the text box that says "Your product or service." The Keyword Planner will provide suggestions based on that seed keyword.

I want to point out that you can change locations. For example, I could narrow this inquiry down to a specific city, such as Austin, Texas, and get data just for Austin. I could also do this for the state of Texas or the United States. The ability to choose specific locations to get data comes in handy when doing research for local SEO if you plan to pursue local SEO clients in the future.

I'm not going to worry about specific locations at this time, though. You should be aiming to receive traffic from all over the world, especially if you want to venture down the Affiliate Marketing path. So, leave the default value set to "All locations."

Next, click "Get ideas." You'll then be taken to the results page.

In the search results page, there will be two tabs: "Ad group ideas" and "Keyword ideas." I don't spend time in the "Ad group ideas" tab because I use Google Keyword Planner for keyword research.

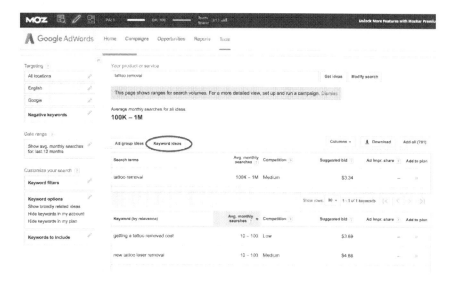

Fig. 05-02

Google Keyword Planner, "Keyword ideas" tab with list of keyword suggestions after searching for "tattoo removal".

The keyword suggestions you want are in the "Keyword (by relevance)" column. To make assessing the keywords easier, sort them by "Average monthly searches." To do so, click on the column name to toggle sorting between ascending and descending order.

The only two columns to be concerned with are the "Keyword (by relevance)" and "Average monthly searches" columns. The other columns are Pay-Per-Click metrics that you shouldn't concern yourself with too much. Even the "Competition" column isn't referring to relevant competition; it refers to how many other Pay-Per-Click advertisers are bidding for the keyword. If that seems a bit too advanced, just know that this is not a dependable measure of how much competition your keyword has.

Here's what a search for the seed keyword "tattoo removal" looks like in Ubersuggest:

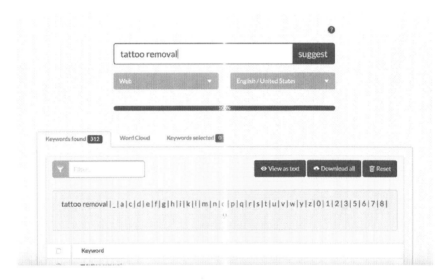

Fig. 05-03
Ubersuggest.io, "tattoo removal" in search field.

Ubersuggest turns a seed keyword into long-tail keywords by adding modifiers. The resulting long-tail keywords are then displayed in alphabetical order of the modifiers.

Ubersuggest is helpful for getting long-tail keyword ideas, especially when you get to the point that you're having a lot of trouble finding new keywords. One thing it can't do is provide the

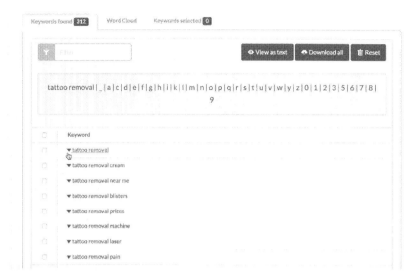

Fig. 05-04

Ubersuggest.io, keyword results after searching for "tattoo removal".

search volume for keywords, but you can bring its suggestions over to Google Keyword Planner to check the search volume *and* get more ideas from Google.

How to Choose What Keywords to Count Out or Target

The ideal keyword has low search volume. So, when faced with the results from your inquiry, eliminate keywords that have more than 1,000 searches a month and pay attention to those that have somewhere between 100 and 1,000 searches a month. You can even regard keywords that have between 10 and 100 searches a month.

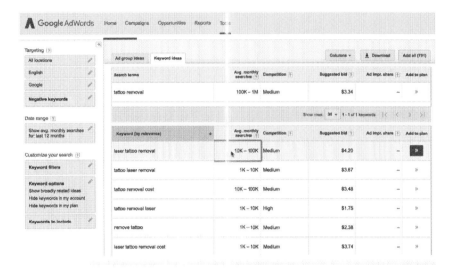

Fig. 05-05

Google Keyword Planner, "Keyword ideas" tab with list of keyword suggestions after searching for "tattoo removal" (sorted by relevance). Note that "laser tattoo removal" gets 10,000 to 100,000 searches a month according to the Average monthly searches *column.*

The results for "laser tattoo removal," which could potentially be a great keyword to rank for, show that it has 10,000 to 100,000 searches a month. As much as I would love to get ranked for this keyword, it's not going to happen (at least not in the timeframe that I would want). This is the kind of keyword that I could probably spend a year or two trying to rank but only creep up on the first page for.

Instead, I'm going to take a keyword with 100 to 1,000 searches a month, like "can tattoos be removed," and see if the competition allows for an opportunity to rank for it.

Fig. 05-06
Google Keyword Planner, "Keyword ideas" tab with list of keyword suggestions after searching for "tattoo removal" (sorted by relevance). Note that the keywords "can tattoos be removed" and "best laser tattoo removal" get 100 to 1,000 searches a month according to the Average monthly searches column.

How to Assess Competition

In order to understand how to assess keyword competition, you need to first understand how to utilize MozBar. For the purposes of this lesson, I'm going to do a Google search using the keyword, "can tattoos be removed." Then, I'm going to walk you through the MozBar metrics to see what the competition looks like.

Fig. 05-07
Google search results for keyword "can tattoos be
removed" showing the MozBar at the top of the page.
Note the settings on the MozBar are for "Google US
non-personalized," which is what we want.

When doing a keyword search on Google, don't add quotation marks because people normally don't add quotes to their search queries. Also, make sure that the MozBar is set to "non-personalized." Before I explain why, I need to tell you about **Google Personalized Search.**

Google Personalized Search is a feature that takes into account both the relevance of each webpage and the websites a user (or someone else using the same browser) has visited through previous search results. As a result, websites you visit more often may get ranked higher than other pages, even though those other pages may be more relevant to your search term.

You can see how this would affect your own keyword research. Your results will be skewed by the sites you've previously visited. To avoid this, you can either use private browsing, which is available in most browsers, or set MozBar to "remove personalization." Either way, the important thing is to not display personalized search results so that you base your decisions on the most accurate data possible.

Fig. 05-08
Google search results for keyword "can tattoos be removed" showing the MozBar on top, scrolled down so that ads are hidden.

The top result for the keyword "can tattoos be removed" is from *WebMD.com*, a highly authoritative site (DA = 95/100). It makes sense that this is the top result because tattoo removal is health-related. It's quite difficult to outrank a site with that kind of authority.

The next result is from *RealSelf.com*, which appears to be a forum for cosmetic surgery patients and doctors. Patients can share their treatment experiences, along with doctor reviews, costs, and honest opinions on which surgeries are worthwhile. Patients, or those considering cosmetic surgery, can also ask questions that real doctors respond to. *RealSelf.com* has a high DA score as well (DA = 71/100).

As mentioned previously, the PA score is what you need to focus on. The WebMD webpage result has a PA score of 72, while the RealSelf webpage result has a PA score of 48.

It's important to note that if you see a result with a PA score of 1 among other results with PA scores of 50 and up, there's either a reporting error from Moz, or this is a localized result (i.e., Moz used your location, indicated by your IP address). For example, when I searched the keyword "can tattoos be removed," one of the results that came up is from a local business called Eraser Clinic, which is the clinic that I go to for my tattoo removal treatments.

Fig. 05-09

Focus on one of the Google search results for "can tattoos be removed" that has a PA score of 1 but is on the first page of the search results.

The likeliest reason Eraser Clinic is shown on the first page of this search result is because of my location. Google thinks this tattoo clinic near me would be helpful. Competition-wise, "can tattoos be removed" is a pretty scary keyword in that the PA scores of ranking pages are high and difficult to beat. I *did* say that it was going to be challenging to find a keyword with ranking pages that have PA scores of 10 or below in today's search climate.

The next metric to consider is how well webpages are optimized for the exact keyword. I mentioned that you can try and look for the exact keyword in the meta title and meta description of the search results.

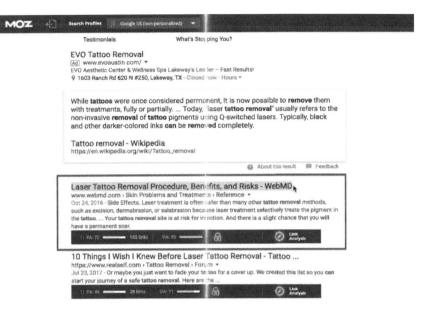

Fig. 05-10

Focus on one of the Google search results for "can tattoos be removed" with the meta title highlighted.

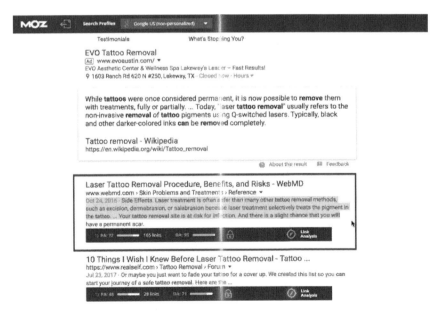

Fig. 05-11

Focus on one of the Google search results for "can tattoos be removed" with the meta description highlighted.

Looking through the search results for my key-word, it seems not one webpage has the exact keyword in either the meta title or meta descrip-tion. I see the keyword broken up throughout the content, but I don't see any of the meta titles or meta descriptions, or even URL slugs, that have the exact keyword. Thus, none of the pages are fully optimized for "can tattoos be removed," which is the only good sign from this search result.

The struggle with using free keyword tools is that selecting a keyword is almost always going to be a tough call. Personally, I'm much more comfortable seeing search results without optimized meta titles and descriptions (in other words, the keyword is not in the meta title or description) and PA scores in the 20s. In these cases, I'm more enthusiastic about selecting and writing for that keyword.

For the keyword "can tattoos be removed," I wouldn't expect to rank if I write an article or post for it based on the PA scores of the other search results. I might add the keyword to my list as a moderate-competition keyword and for reconsideration when my website authority builds up in the coming months, but for now I don't think this is going to work out. It takes a lot of time to rule out even just one keyword. As time goes on, though, you'll find that it gets easier.

Let's use "best laser tattoo removal" and see if we have better luck with it. According to Google

Keyword Planner, this keyword also has around 100 to 1,000 monthly searches.

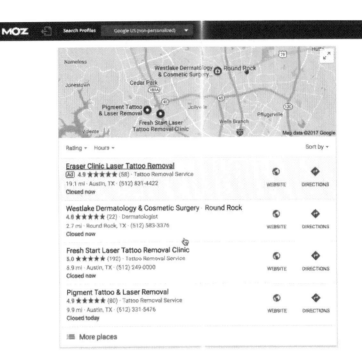

Fig. 05-12

Focus on localized Google search results for "best laser tattoo removal" with local tattoo removal clinics plus their locations on a map.

Google recognizes this keyword as a local-oriented search phrase. When a user searches "best laser tattoo removal," Google thinks they are looking for the best laser tattoo removal clinic nearby, not the best type of laser tattoo removal. Thus, I wouldn't even look at this keyword extensively because although it's possible to get ranked somewhere at the bottom half of page one, the top half of page one for this term is going to be dominated by local results. That's not going to be worth my time.

The same localized search results can be observed if I inquire about the keywords "laser for tattoo removal" and "tattoo removal clinic."

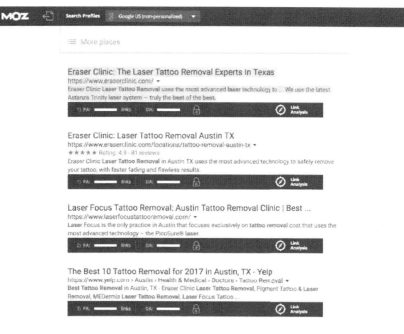

Fig. 05-13
Focus on the rest of the Google search results for "best laser tattoo removal." Note again the local search results included, such as websites of tattoo removal clinics in Austin, as well as Yelp and Reddit results that are about tattoo removal clinics in Austin.

Notice that these results have low PA scores; again, don't automatically assume that you'll be able to rank for a keyword because the other pages have low PA scores.

A keyword that Google Keyword Planner suggested is "getting a tattoo removed cost." Whenever you see a keyword that doesn't grammatically make sense, skip over it. Optimizing an article for a grammatically incorrect phrase is difficult. Readers can always tell when something is off about your article, and it's hard to gain peoples' trust when you have atrocious grammar. Plus, Google's algorithms are beginning to understand when an article is written in poor English.

Now I'm going to try the keyword "permanent tattoo removal price" and see what I get from that.

Fig. 05-14
Focus on the first few Google search results for "permanent tattoo removal price." Note the slightly lower PA scores compared to the search results for "can tattoos be removed".

There are no local results, which is a good sign. Some of the other pages do have fairly high PA scores, but they're not as high as the first keyword we were looking at ("can tattoos be removed"). Plus, none of the results on the first page have "permanent tattoo removal price" in their meta titles or meta descriptions. So, this is a keyword I would actually write for.

I could write an article titled "Permanent Tattoo Removal Price: How Much Does Laser Tattoo Removal Cost?" and rank for more than one keyword. It would take a fair amount of research on my end because not all tattoos cost the same per session. I know how much *my* particular tattoo cost is per session, but that doesn't necessarily apply to all tattoos. Many people have tattoos that are much smaller than mine, while other people have tattoos that are much bigger.

How to Organize the Data You've Gathered

Free keyword tools don't provide straightforward ways to store the information you discover, so you'll have to take note of everything yourself.

I recommend creating a spreadsheet with the following columns:

- *Keyword* – This column would serve to keep track of each keyword you find.

- *Search Volume* – This column would serve to keep track of each keyword's monthly search volume.

- *Average PA Score* – This column would serve to keep track of each keyword's Page Authority score.

- *Optimized for KW?* – This column would serve to indicate if the exact keyword was found in the meta title and meta description.

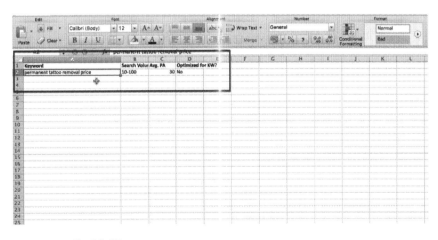

Fig. 05-15
Spreadsheet with columns Keyword, Search Volume,
Avg. PA, *and* Optimized for KW?

As you go through the process of researching keywords, fill in each column with the corresponding information when you find one that works. Continue this process until you find at least 10 keywords that meet the same criteria discussed in section 5.4 of this chapter.

I know it seems daunting to go through the process 10 times, but this is what it takes to create posts that attract the right visitors using a free keyword tool. Whenever you feel overwhelmed, take a deep breath and remind yourself of the big picture.

Remember that everything need not be absolutely perfect and that you're doing the best you can. If you can't afford premium keyword tools, work with what you've got and stick with it. Don't feel bad, crappy, or like you're doomed. You don't have time for that. Practice and get really good at everything I've taught you. Focus on doing your best and putting out excellent quality content. Keep at it and you're going to see results.

5.6 Finding Keywords Quickly and Easily Using Premium Keyword Tools

Some Notes About Paid Keyword Tools

Paid keyword tools are certainly nice to have, but **they're not at all required** to succeed in this industry. Awesome keyword research can be done using free keyword tools and the techniques taught in the previous section. Don't beat yourself up or stress about not being able to purchase premium tools; you're not going to fail just because you can't afford a premium keyword tool.

That said, premium keyword tools make keyword research a breeze, saving you plenty of time that can be used to actually write and optimize content. If you have the extra income to invest after hosting and domain name set up, **a keyword tool is the next best thing to invest in.**

Based on my years of experience using both free and premium tools, I guarantee that you're going to set yourself up for success much better, and sooner, if you invest in a premium keyword tool.

Pros and Cons of Using Premium Keyword Tools

Pro: Helpful Competition Data at a Glance

MozBar is a very helpful but laborious tool to use. Premium keyword tools make it unnecessary to go through the steps for MozBar because they do it for you.

Pro: Majestic Metrics

Majestic metrics are more reliable than Moz metrics. For years, Moz DA and PA were the industry standards when it came to website authority. However, for the past couple of years, they've been overtaken by Majestic, which uses Trust Flow (TF) and Citation Flow (CF) instead. Moz metrics are still useful, but as far as measuring website authority and keyword competition, Majestic's TF and CF are the best indicators for Internet Marketers doing keyword research and SEO.

Pro: More Holistic and Reliable Data

Because Majestic's metrics are more reliable than Moz's, you can expect a much more accurate representation of the competition you face. Plus, all the data is in one place; no need to open several different tools or create spreadsheets to track the data. As a result, the information you gather is going to be more reliable on the whole because it's not pieced together.

Pro: Save a Ton of Time

Moving back and forth between tools and assessing each keyword and search result page individually adds up to a great deal of time that you'll save when using a premium tool.

Con: Premium Keyword Tools Are Costly

At the time of this publication, the annual plans for premium keyword tools range from $300 to $500. Frankly, it's not a cheap investment, but it's one that's worth making if you can swing it.

The Best Paid Keyword Research Tool

There are a number of paid keyword research tools available, but the best keyword tool I recommend is Long Tail Pro (*LongTailPro.com*), a tool recommended by many Internet Marketers who have been in the industry for a long time.

Long Tail Pro simplifies a lot of really complex data into Key Performance Indicators (KPIs) so you can view it all at a glance. This cuts keyword research time by 90%, if not more.

Long Tail Pro includes plenty of other features such as **Rank Tracker**, a feature that monitors your search results ranking, and **Long Tail University**, an in-depth and advanced course on SEO and keyword research.

Setting Up Long Tail Pro

When you sign up for Long Tail Pro's free trial, you'll be taken to the homepage (see Fig. 05-16).

You'll need to first add a project to view your dashboard. To add a project, click the plus sign to the left of the "Default" dropdown menu, enter a project name, and click "Add" (see Fig. 05-17).

Fig. 05-16
Long Tail Pro homepage. Note the plus symbol next to
"Default" at the top of the page.

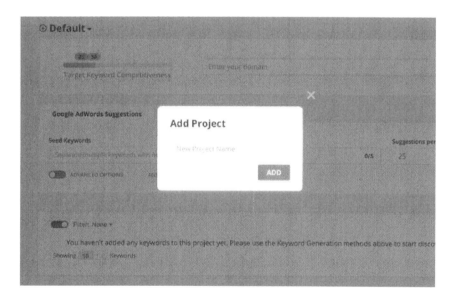

Fig. 05-17
Long Tail Pro homepage with "Add Project" modal window.

The next step after creating a project is entering
a domain name. Enter your domain name where
it says "Enter your domain" and click on the "Add"
button.

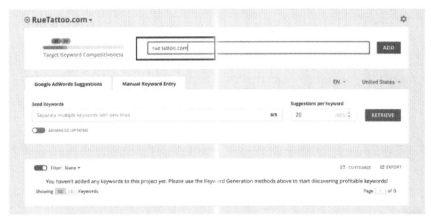

Fig. 05-18
Long Tail Pro homepage with "Enter your domain name"
field filled in.

The screen should look like this after you click the "Add" button:

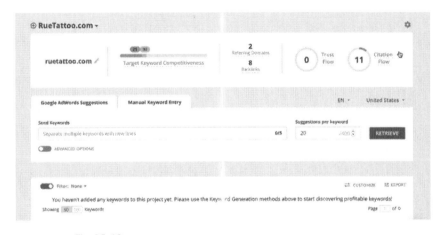

Fig. 05-19
Long Tail Pro homepage, Inside Project dashboard, showing
Target Keyword Competitiveness ideal range, Trust Flow,
and Citation Flow for the added domain.

Your KPIs are all in one place where the range of target keyword competitiveness, domain trust flow, and your domain citation flow can clearly be seen.

How to Use Long Tail Pro for Keyword Research

The next step is to do the actual keyword research.

There are two options to do this: either select the default option (which is to have Long Tail Pro search Google AdWords Keyword Planner for keyword suggestions from a seed keyword) or enter keywords manually. For the purposes of this training, I'm going to use the default option.

 Before I dig in, though, I want to call your attention to the fact that **depending on your subscription plan, you only have a certain number of keyword searches a month**, ranging from 10,000 to 60,000. Long Tail Pro doesn't count how many times you click "Retrieve" as a search; it counts *each* of the keyword suggestions as one keyword search. The maximum number of keyword suggestions Long Tail Pro retrieves at a time is 400.

If you choose to keep the limit set to 400, you'll burn through your monthly allotted keyword searches very quickly. A good number of suggestions to start with is 25. This will give you fewer, but more relevant, suggestions from more seed keywords instead of several irrelevant suggestions from only a handful of seed keywords.

On the bright side, once a keyword suggestion is retrieved, it is saved until deleted from the project.

That means if you want to see a particular suggestion again, there's no need to retrieve suggestions again. Long Tail Pro's ability to save keyword suggestions means you save on searches each month. As a result, every time you input a new seed keyword, the keyword suggestions are added onto the previous ones.

I'll do a search using "laser tattoo removal" as the seed keyword to show what it looks like when a search is done:

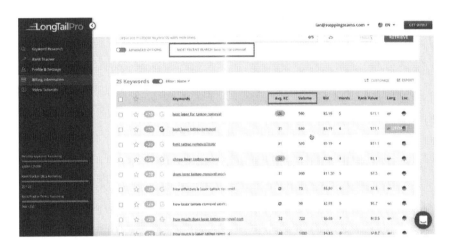

Fig. 05-20
Long Tail Pro homepage, Google AdWords Suggestions, seed keyword "laser tattoo removal", 25 suggestions per seed keyword. The columns Average Keyword Competitiveness (Avg. KC) and Volume are the most useful.

Another helpful feature of Long Tail Pro is the color coding of the Average KC values, depending on the Target Keyword Competitiveness suggested based on your domain. If the Target Keyword

Competitiveness value is within the recommended range, it shows up as green. If it's beyond the suggested range, but still within an acceptable threshold, it will be yellow. If it's way outside the suggested range, then it's not highlighted at all.

If your website is brand new, I wouldn't recommend going outside the 15 to 20 KC value range. For my domain, Long Tail Pro recommends below a 25 value. I *can* go up to the 25 to 30 range, but from experience, lower is better.

This keyword list can be sorted by average keyword competitiveness. I recommend sorting your list this way so you can see the lowest hanging fruit at the top.

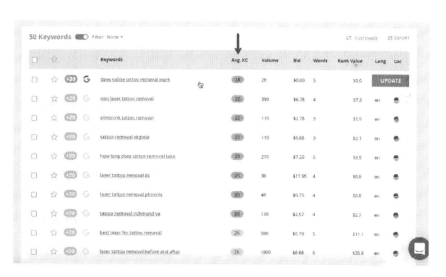

Fig. 05-21
Long Tail Pro homepage, Google AdWords Suggestions,
sorted by Avg. KC in ascending order.

Long Tail Pro: Competition Analysis Page

Clicking on a keyword will show the Competition Analysis page for that keyword. The Competition Analysis page contains information about the monthly search volume of that keyword as well as the metrics for the top ten results in Google when it's searched.

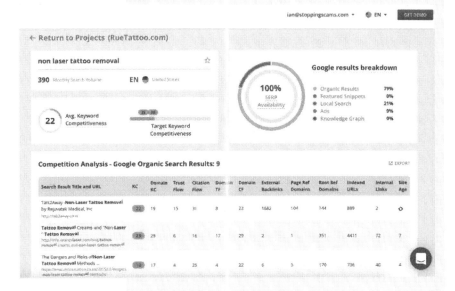

Fig. 05-22
Long Tail Pro Competition Analysis page for keyword "non laser tattoo removal." Note the "Monthly Search Volume" below the keyword, "Google results breakdown" at the top right, and the "Competition Analysis" table at the bottom half of the page. Note also the columns in the "Competition Analysis" table that are the most important for keyword research: Search Result title and URL, KC, and Trust Flow. Domain KC, and Domain Trust Flow are worth looking at but are also much less important.

When using free tools, you have to go back and forth between Google Keyword Planner and

Mozbar to check the search volume and competition of a keyword. Long Tail Pro eliminates those steps and provides all the information you need in one table on a single page.

Aside from the monthly search volume, the Competition Analysis page also displays what percent of the results are organic search results and which are local search results. In order to gather this information using free keyword tools, you need to do a Google search yourself and run the risk that the keyword you're researching is treated by Google as a local search query.

Long Tail Pro instantly provides the information needed to determine whether or not you're going to be competing against local businesses. The keyword "non laser tattoo removal" has a local result percentage of 21%, which isn't too bad. However, the fact that this keyword has a local result percentage means you will still have a bit of a disadvantage.

Long Tail Pro: Trust Flow and Citation Flow

The next metric to focus on is the Trust Flow (TF) of your competition. Majestic's TF measures the quality of **backlinks** to a site. Backlinks are links from outside domains that point to pages on your domain, essentially linking back from their domain to yours. Fairly new or small sites don't have a lot of domains referring to them, but high-authority websites are more likely to be linked to by other high-authority websites. Trust Flow scores the quality of those backlinks.

When you check the Competition Analysis of a keyword and see that the **average TF is around 10 to 15**, that's a sign that you can probably outrank your competitors for that keyword. However, if your website is new, and TF values are around 20 to 25 (or higher), then it's wise to research other keywords because it's difficult to outrank competitors for keywords with a TF value of 20 or above. The exceptions to this are high-competition niches where everyone's TF scores are in the 50s to 70s.

Citation Flow (CF), by contrast, measures the *total* number of backlinks to a page without factoring in the quality of sites that link back to the domain. TF measures *quality*, while CF measures *influence*. Therefore, TF is the main metric to look at when determining competition because Google ranks domains with trustworthy backlinks regardless of the actual number of backlinks a domain has.

Long Tail Pro also measures how competitive the top search results for a keyword are. Aside from the TF, CF, and other backlink data, the page title and URL are also taken into consideration. If a keyword is in other pages' title and URL, that means those pages are optimized for that keyword; this is going to boost the competitiveness of those pages.

The Competition Analysis page makes deciding whether or not a keyword is worth writing for a much quicker process than maneuvering between many different tools. The time you save with premium tools is extremely valuable, so if you have the extra investment, it's worth spending on a premium keyword tool.

Chapter 5 Summary

‖‖

- A **keyword** is a word or phrase someone searches in a search engine when they're seeking information. Keyword research is fundamental to success in Internet Marketing.

- Traditionally, Internet Marketers favor keywords that have high search volume and low competition, but this is not a feasible way to select keywords anymore.

- For early-stage blogs and websites that have little to zero marketing budget, creating content focused on dozens of keywords that have lower search volume has a greater likelihood of success than focusing on a single higher search volume keyword over the same period of time.

- To use keywords to ignite your content, find one or two keywords that you want to target in an article, write a high-quality post around that keyword, and optimize your post for the target keyword.

- An ideal keyword should have 30 to 100 searches a month and be low competition. Remember to always ask yourself: *is the person who's searching for this keyword in my target audience?*

- When building your keyword list, be aware of qualified versus unqualified traffic. **Qualified traffic** is traffic that converts (i.e., makes you money) and **unqualified traffic** is worthless traffic.

- Just because a keyword has search volume that you could potentially get rankings for doesn't mean it's worth your time or it's going to make you money.

- The main advantage of free keyword tools is that they're free.

- The disadvantage of using free keyword tools is that data on competition isn't as substantial, accurate, or reliable as that from premium tools. Additionally, using free keyword tools takes more time.

- The Best Free Keyword Tools are Google AdWords Keyword Planner, Keyword.io, UberSuggest.io, and MozBar.

- Important Google Keyword Planner metrics include Keyword Suggestions and Average Monthly Searches (ideal search volume = 100 to 1,000 or 10 to 100 searches a month). Eliminate keywords that have more than 1,000 searches a month.

- Important MozBar metrics include Page Authority (PA) and Domain Authority (DA).

- When reviewing search result pages, focus on whether the results don't include pages with the exact keyword in their meta title and description, do include pages from question-and-answer sites, and do include pages hosted by free blog platforms.

- A general step-by-step guide to using free keyword tools:

  o Use Google Keyword Planner and Ubersuggest.io to get keyword suggestions.

  o Use Google Keyword Planner to research search volume. Weed out keywords with search volumes greater than 1,000 and focus on what's left.

- Eliminate grammatically incorrect keywords.

- Use Google Search and do a non-personalized search of your candidate keyword. Examine search results using the criteria described above.

- Take note of the ones that have potential using a spreadsheet.

- Advantages of using premium keyword tools include reliable data on competition that's available at a glance, scores that are based on Majestic metrics (which are more reliable than Moz metrics) and saved time.

- The disadvantage of using premium keyword tools is that they require a significant investment.

- The Best Premium Keyword Tool is Long Tail Pro.

- Important metrics to look at when using Long Tail Pro are Average Keyword Competitiveness (KC) and Trust Flow (TF):

  - Average KC = ideal value is 15 to 20 (or lower)

  - TF = ideal value is around 10 to 15 (lower is better)

Chapter 6: Writing High-Quality Content That Gets Ranked

You read it everywhere and hear it all the time:

"Content is king."

"Make sure to write high-quality content."

"High-quality content is the key to success in Internet Marketing."

What does all of that actually mean, though?

In this chapter, I'll explain EXACTLY why high-quality content is so important and how to create it quickly and efficiently.

6.1 How to Create High-Quality Content: "Inch Wide, Mile Deep"

I've stated repeatedly in previous chapters how essential high-quality content is to an Internet Marketing business, and now it's finally time to discuss it in detail.

Technically, you don't need high-quality content to get ranked. If you have really sophisticated SEO skills and know how to game Google without getting caught, you can *maybe* get away with subpar content.

But for the average person who's playing by the rules, high-quality content is an absolute must for any Internet Marketing business.

Why You Need High-Quality Content

I've discussed how an Internet Marketing business is cumulative and how your efforts will stack on top of each other. Content is an important step that will help amplify your business' success. Focusing on high-quality content will ultimately make succeeding easier and happen quicker.

I also want to emphasize that when I say "content," it doesn't necessarily mean written content. Other types of content you can study and create are videos and podcasts.

I'm Not Here to Teach You How to Write

This chapter is not about how to become a good writer. I won't be focusing on proper English grammar or punctuation or how to compose a well-written sentence. I'm NOT an English teacher. If you plan to build a business with written content and you can write in English, *you're going to be fine*. Writing imperfectly is not that big of a deal in Internet Marketing. There is always time to learn how to improve your writing at a basic level. Plenty of materials available online can teach you proper grammar, punctuation, and spelling. If you *are* an incredible writer, everything will fall into place more quickly for you. At the end of the day, though, **you don't need to aim for perfection**.

Take me as an example: I've always been a decent writer, which I owe in part to my grandmother who was an English teacher for 32 years. When I first started writing blog posts 10 years ago, I would spend an entire day writing an article that, today, I can knock out in a couple of hours. "Practice makes perfect" may be a cliché, but it's true. Every time you sit down and write an article or post, you're working towards improvement.

The Key to Producing High-Quality Content

The key to producing high-quality content (whether it's written, video, or audio) is to add value to your followers' lives. Focusing on value above anything else will ensure that your content is engaging and informative. This applies to each content format and niche.

I've learned a lot in this industry over the years and know I'm providing the highest quality training I could ever provide by focusing on sharing everything I've learned in this book. My hope is to help readers achieve the same, or even greater, success that I'm experiencing now.

"Inch Wide, Mile Deep"

A common mistake people make is trying to write everything there is to write about for a broad topic. The result is a piece of content that's too watered down to add real value.

The right approach to creating content is: **"inch wide, mile deep."** Focus on a tiny segment within a broad topic (inch wide) and flesh it out (mile deep). This is the best rule of thumb for writing high-quality content.

For my tattoo removal website, for example, I wouldn't write about and cram every topic regarding laser tattoo removal, such as how much it hurts, the cost, the technology, etc., into a single blog post. Instead, I'd write individual blog posts for each of the smaller topics within the broad topic of tattoo removal (inch wide) and flesh out very specific questions or pain points in each one (mile deep).

There are certain exceptions to this rule. Once these individual blog posts are published, I could create a longer article to serve as an overview of a broad topic, such as tattoo removal, that summarizes important points from each of the individual posts. In this longer article I would link out to each in-depth article so readers could find more information on that specific topic. These types of articles are known as **cornerstone content**, content that forms the foundation or basis of a website. This doesn't contradict the "inch wide, mile deep" approach; it's a necessary exception so you can have a major piece that anchors minor posts on your blog.

High-Quality Content Alone Will Make Your Business a Success

Every website needs a foundation of at least seven to 10 pieces of high-quality content before promotion. The idea here is to have your core pages, which were discussed in Chapter 4, and at least seven to 10 high-quality blog posts.

You could get away with promoting your site with only four or five extremely high-quality articles, but that may hurt your promotional efforts. If you send a website with five articles or less to people, it won't matter how high quality the articles are; that website is going to look brand new. It's a stretch for your website to be seen as an authority in your niche with only two or three published posts.

At this point, focus on laying the groundwork for your website by creating seven to 10 high-quality articles that serve as the basis for the rest of your content.

6.2 Preparing Content and Creating an Outline

IIIIIIIIIIIIIIIIIIIIIIIIIIIIIIIIIIIIIIIIIIIIIIIIIIIIIIIIIIIIIIIIIIIIIIIIIIIIIIIIIIIIIIIIIIIIIIIIIIIII

This section will discuss how to prepare to write high-quality content. There are different approaches to writing content, but I've found that creating an outline makes the writing process more efficient.

Step 1: Do Your Research

Before creating an outline, you'll need to **research the topic extensively**. Keyword research is a great starting point but doing research for an article is very different. This is where expertise comes in handy; the more experience you have in a niche and the topic you're writing about, the less time you're going to spend doing research. The opposite is true for niches and topics you're interested in but know little about.

Make sure to only gather information from credible sources. The last thing you want to do is spend hours researching and gathering inaccurate information about a topic. Keep researching until you're certain the information you're going to put out is correct and factual. This is important for your authority and credibility down the road.

Step 2: Create an Outline

Creating an outline will dramatically boost your productivity.

Think back to essay writing in school. An essay is composed of **an introduction, a conclusion, and a body with at least three main points** that are discussed in detail. The same structure works very well for blog posts.

The three main points of your post need to address your readers' pain points and questions head-on. Remember, you need to add value to your readers' lives, so make those main points relevant and helpful to them.

At this early stage, balance the quality of your content with how often you publish a post. In terms of SEO, you want your website to be updated often. Some people post 800-word, sometimes even 500-word, articles frequently, but it's nearly impossible to provide value with content this short because it barely scratches the surface of a given topic. Even if the article were entertaining and well written, the substance would almost certainly be lacking.

By contrast, some people think the only way to establish authority is to put out 5,000 or 10,000-word articles. To a degree, they're right; long-form articles are a great way to establish authority. However, in the early days when you're establishing your sea legs, you don't want to spend several days composing gigantic pieces of content.

Striking a balance between the frequency and quality of posts should be incorporated into the initial content strategy. The ideal length of high-quality posts that can still be published fairly often is **1,200 to 1,500 words**. In time, as you build authority with 1,200-word articles, you'll begin to produce articles with 2,000 or even 5,000 words to establish authority in your niche.

How Much Does Tattoo Removal Hurt? An Honest Patient's Experience

Introduction — My experiences from a GIANT tattoo removal

Point #1 — What people vs. what it ACTUALLY feels like
"It feels like someone snapping a rubber band against your skin"
What it actually feels like
Hurts a lot more than getting a tattoo

Point #2 — More Painful, but Much Faster
Even a huge tattoo like mine only takes 15-30 minutes per session; smaller tattoos can take as little as a couple of minutes
More pain can be a good thing (more ink removed, but...
The wrong technology or an untrained technician will cause unnecessary damage which equals more pain
Don't pay an expensive dermatologist unnecessarily; make sure to get _____ type of laser and certified, experienced technicians

Point # 3 — Pain relief options pre-treatment and during treatment
Numbing ointments like Hush or Aspercreme; still hurts but makes the sessions much more bearable
Getting a topical anesthetic prescription from your PCP
Ibuprofen (or whatever the acceptable NSAID is); do NOT use anything that thins blood
Relaxing + mind over matter; meditation

Point #4 — Pain relief options post-treatment
The same NSAID as pre-treatment
A good ice compress
Loose clothing
A very tiny amount of patience — it'll pass within a day or two

Conclusion — the pain is temporary, your dislike for your tattoo will last forever
Treat it like a band-aid and schedule an appointment

Fig. 06-01
Example of an outline made while writing a blog post.

Above is an example of an outline I made for a blog post on *RueTattoo.com*. There may be typos in the outline, and that's fine. Outlines are internal documents meant to improve your productivity, not to be published. As you can see, this outline contains an introduction, four major points, and a conclusion.

Two things are evident from this outline: I've done my research before composing it and writing it took some time, but it's time spent doing something that will save you time when creating the content. Once the outline is complete and you begin writing the article, you can write the introduction and major points without getting confused or not knowing what your next point is because it's all in the outline! This makes your research and writing processes so much more efficient.

Other Things to Remember About Writing Content

One thing I've learned throughout the years is to **never edit while writing**. What I mean is that you should never do major revisions in your article while you're in the middle of writing it. Trying to get everything perfect during the first draft dramatically hurts your efficiency. The more practical thing to do is to write what comes to mind during your first draft until it's done. *Then* go back and edit and revise as needed.

Another lesson I've learned is to **type drafts into a plain-text editor** such as Notepad in Windows or Notes in Mac. Typing a draft into a word-processing software, like Microsoft Word or Pages for Mac, will cause problems when the content is copy and pasted into the built-in editor of WordPress.

The time to proofread and edit your work, apply the necessary formatting (e.g., emphasis on certain words, headlines, subheadings, bullet points, etc.), and insert relevant images is when the content has been pasted into WordPress. Leave the cosmetic tweaks for *after* you've drafted your content. This allows you to focus on one thing at a time, from the most important to the least.

6.3 How to Format Content for the Web

You have an outline ready and a plain-text editor fired up, but there are some things you need to know before you start writing your content.

What Should Web Content Look Like?

It seems superficial to be concerned with the appearance of content, however, you need to remember that websites and blogs are also visual media. People are naturally attracted to great visuals.

Keep in mind that there's a big difference between web content and print media. Even though they're both visual media, people interact with them in different ways. Applying the formatting and style that is characteristic of print media (magazines, newspapers, books, etc.) to your website is going to make for a terrible user experience and hinder the success of your website. After all, if people don't like looking at your website, how are they expected to engage with the content?

Break Down Paragraphs into Smaller Chunks

In books, authors can get away with boxes of text. Writing boxes of text in blog posts or articles will look overwhelming to even to the most avid reader.

Avoid Stylish and Hard to Read Fonts

Sans-serif fonts are easier to read on a screen while serif fonts are easier to read on paper. The details and science behind this are beyond the scope of this book, so I won't be going into detail about it. However, please keep this in mind as you begin creating your content. The example shows a great comparison between sans-serif and serif font.

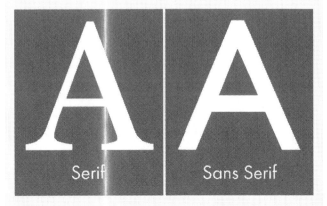

Fig. 06-02
Serif (left) versus sans-serif font (right). Notice the slight extra elements, called serifs, on the legs of the letter "A" to the left.

Never Justify Your Text

Another difference between web content and print media is that text alignment in print is almost always justified. This is because text in print, especially in magazines and newspapers, is usually formatted in columns, and justifying text makes the edges nice and neat. However, web content is almost always formatted in a single-column, so it's not important for the edges to align well. When web content is justified, gaps between the words become bigger and interrupt the reading experience. This effect looks even worse on smaller devices, like smartphones and tablets. Plus, justified text is a nightmare to code. So, it's best to never justify the text of your articles.

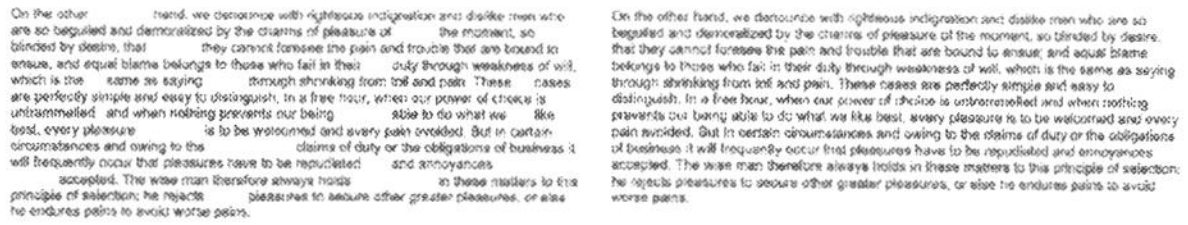

Fig. 06-03

Justified (left) versus left-aligned text (right). Note how the gaps in between words on the justified text is distracting and interrupts the natural flow of the eye.

Strike a Balance Between SEO and User Experience (UX)

To boost your on-page SEO and lay the foundations to get ranked for your chosen keyword, insert those keywords into the text of your article. However, don't overdo it to the point that your articles are unreadable and UX suffers. Sacrifice UX and your prospects of success go down the drain.

Insert Images Throughout the Article

Paragraphs should be broken up so readers aren't facing walls of text and adding images can help with that. Images add visual appeal to your content. Just make sure the images you select are relevant to the subject of your blog post and not just there to look pretty.

6.4 Where to Find Free High-Quality and Royalty-Free Images

This is not an exhaustive list; there are many more resources available and plenty of articles online that compile the best ones. What I'm going to share are my favorite resources and *why* I like using them so you know what to look for if you opt to venture outside this list.

My Favorite Image Resources

Each of these resources offers royalty-free images that you can download, use, and alter in any way without providing credit.

 Pixabay.com: Pixabay has been my go-to resource for years. There are plenty of beautiful images available, and the search function does a great job of finding what you're looking for. The only minor issue I have with Pixabay are the corny graphics thrown in with the high-quality images.

 Unsplash.com: The great thing about Unsplash is that the images are contributions from photographers all over the world and are thus stunning and one-of-a-kind. The search function is not as powerful as Pixabay's, but it's workable.

 Burst by Shopify.com: Burst is a fairly recent but equally remarkable image resource. The selection is smaller than Pixabay's and Unsplash's, but the images are professional quality.

Image Attribution: What You Need to Know

The reason why anyone can use images from these websites without needing to attribute or give credit is because they're licensed under the Creative Commons CC0. To summarize the legalese, **Creative Common CC0** means that the people who upload their photos to these sites waive their copyright to the images. Therefore, anyone can download, use, and adapt these photos for any purpose, both commercial and non-commercial, without having to credit the source or the original creator.

If you use images from other websites (such as Flickr or ones found on Google Images) in your content, they may not all be licensed the same. Discussing digital image licenses in detail is too broad and off-topic, but just know that **you shouldn't use an image or video off the internet without determining if it's protected by copyright.** If the images *are* free to use, there may be certain conditions to be able to use them, such as giving credit or linking back to the original source.

It's simpler to stick to the resources mentioned above. If you absolutely can't find what you're looking for from these three sites, make sure to check the terms and conditions of a different site and the photos it offers before downloading anything.

It can be tempting to use the photos you find on Google. You might think, *"What's the big deal? It's the internet. If I can see it on my browser, I should be able to use it, right?"*

The big deal is that if you happen to mess with the wrong website owner or author, and they decide to pursue action against you, your website can be shut down, temporarily or permanently. Worst case scenario, you'll end up in court. Trust me on this; take intellectual property laws seriously.

6.5 Everything You Need to Know About On-Page SEO

I've briefly discussed Search Engine Optimization in previous chapters, but now it's time to really delve into on-page SEO.

I'd like to point out that the following information is merely a summary of the essential concepts you need to know when starting out. A comprehensive discussion of on-page SEO requires a book of its own. This section is only meant to provide enough knowledge of the basics to start applying them to your website.

Why Learning On-Page SEO Is Necessary

On-page SEO is essential to be ranked highly in Search Engine Results Pages (SERPs). You want your pages to rank highly for the keywords you're trying to rank so that more people will visit your website.

Given your limited time and resources, it's only logical to try and optimize for the best and most widely used search engine out there. Even though the figures vary, Google is the undisputed leader in the search engine market (some statistics state 65%, while others state as high as 87%), so it'll seem that we're doing everything to please Google.

Which Elements to Focus On

*VERY Important Note: Shortly before we published this book, Wordpress **dramatically** redesigned their visual page and post editor, so your screens won't quite match up with those in this book by default.*

You can switch back to Wordpress' "classic editor" very easily, which will make all of your screens when drafting pages or posts on your website match up with those within this book.

*Just search the internet using a phrase along the lines of "**how to change back to Wordpress classic editor**" and you should be able to find multiple articles and* *videos that will walk you through this process step-by-step in less than five minutes.*

The most important aspects of your article to insert your keyword into are the post title, meta title, meta description, and URL slug. Get your keyword in every single one of these elements and your post is as good as 80% optimized.

Every post needs a **post title** or headline. This is what your readers see when they click on the URL for your post on SERPs and when they read it.

I touched on the **meta title and meta description** in Chapter 5. These are elements that are shown

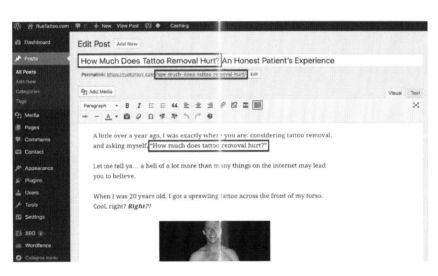

Fig. 06-04

WordPress Dashboard, Posts, Add New, Add New Post, Visual Editor. Note that the Page Title at the top of the post ("How Much Does Tattoo Removal Hurt? An Honest Patient's Experience"), the URL slug, also called the Permalink (https://ruetattoo.com/how-much-does-tattoo-removal-hurt/), and the first paragraph of the article all contain the focus keyword "how much does tattoo removal hurt."

on SERPs. Your meta title can be different from the actual post title, which I'll show below.

I also discussed the **URL slug** briefly in the previous chapter. This is how your readers actually go into your post.

Other elements of your post to aim to use the keyword in are one other header (aside from your page title), image alt tags (when you can), and throughout your content (where appropriate).

I'll show you what each one of these elements look like in WordPress, specifically in the Visual Editor and in the Yoast SEO plugin section.

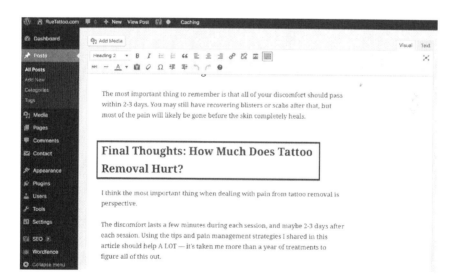

Fig. 06-05
WordPress Dashboard, Posts, Add New, Add New Post,
Visual Editor. Note that the Heading 2 subheader ("Final
Thoughts: How Much Does Tattoo Removal Hurt?") contains
the focus keyword "how much does tattoo removal hurt?"

It's good to include your focus keyword in one of the subheaders, but it can sometimes be difficult to do in a way that makes sense.

Pro Tip: include the keyword in your conclusion subheader (e.g., "final thoughts," "final words," or simply "conclusion").

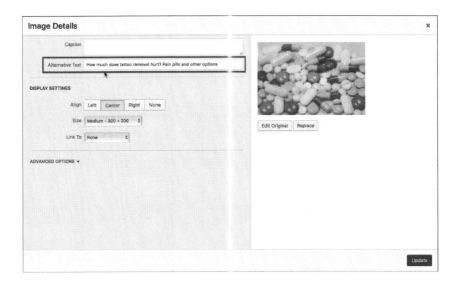

Fig. 06-06
WordPress Dashboard, Posts, Add New, Add New Post, "Image Details" modal window. Note that "Alternative Text" ("How much does tattoo removal hurt? Pain pills and other options") contains the focus keyword "how much does tattoo removal hurt."

Another recommendation is to include your focus keyword in the alternative text, commonly known as the alt tag, of one of your images. The purpose of the alt tag is to describe the images placed on your site for the visually impaired. Their computer will read out this text and thus give them an idea of what your image contains.

The alt tag is also shown when image downloading is forbidden by a particular browser, or if a network connection is slow and images don't load properly. You may have a bit of difficulty including your focus keyword in the alt tag in a way that makes sense. If this is the case, you can include it in the alt tag of your post's featured image.

Yoast SEO Plugin

Yoast SEO is the best SEO plugin available, and it will make optimizing posts and pages for search engines much easier.

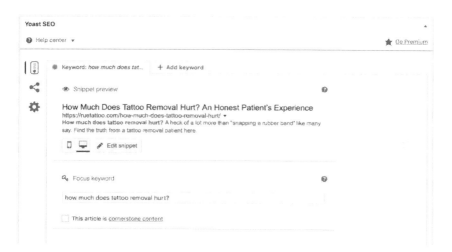

Fig. 06-07

WordPress Dashboard, Posts, Add New, Add New Post, Yoast SEO. Note the meta title ("How Much Does Tattoo Removal Hurt? An Honest Patient's Experience"), URL slug (https://ruetattoo.com/how-much-does-tattoo-removal-hurt/), and meta description ("How much does tattoo removal hurt? A heck of a lot more than 'snapping a rubber band' like many say. Find the truth from a tattoo removal patient here."), as well as the "Focus keyword" field.

301

In WordPress, the meta title can be different from the post title, and you can edit both the meta title and meta description through the Yoast SEO section located below the Visual Editor (see Fig. 06-07).

The "Focus Keyword" field is where to enter the keyword you're trying to optimize. Yoast SEO will then assess your post and determine whether the SEO for the post is good or needs improvement.

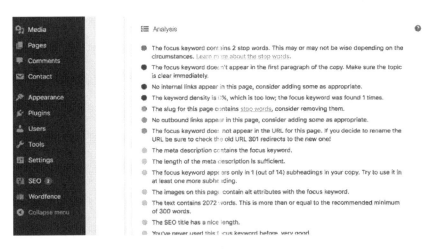

Fig. 06-08
WordPress Dashboard, Posts, Add New, Add New Post, Yoast SEO Analysis.

The "Analysis" section displays what has been done well, what has been done satisfactorily, and what needs to improve. These indicators point you in the right direction, especially for the major elements described earlier. However, take all of this insight with a grain of salt because Yoast SEO isn't perfect.

From the image above, you can see that Yoast claims the focus keyword isn't in the first paragraph, when I'm absolutely sure I put it there. Yoast also claims that my keyword density appears to be 0%. To be fair, the focus keyword ("How much does tattoo removal hurt?") is difficult to naturally insert within a post. Keep in mind that you don't need to place the exact keyword in your content if it doesn't make sense to do so. It's best to prioritize content quality over how many times the exact keyword is mentioned.

Contextual Keywords Matter

When using keywords in the body of your content, it's important to remember not to use the exact phrase if it doesn't make sense. Google's algorithms have become sophisticated enough to recognize the context of a keyword. You can still rank in SERPs if the algorithms sense closely related phrases and synonyms of a keyword were used in the content.

However, this only works if you're actually writing relevant, high-quality content around a focus keyword. If you're not consciously inserting the keyword, you'll tend to use phrases that are synonymous or contextually related. So, remember, **if you're truly producing high-quality content around a focus keyword, you'll still manage to rank in SERPs even if the exact keyword isn't used often throughout the content.**

Let me explain with an example focus keyword I want to optimize: *"how much does tattoo removal* hurt." I may only be able to use that exact phrase a few times throughout my post, so writing a high-quality article means I'll use phrases like *"tattoo removal hurts"* or *"pain management"* or *"pain relief."* Each of these contextual phrases, that are closely related to my focus keyword, are then picked up by Google. Google's algorithms know those phrases are related to the keyword I optimized my post for.

The bottom line is that if you're having trouble fitting an exact keyword in your post, then do your best to use close synonyms and related phrases instead so that your content doesn't turn out robotic and off-putting.

6.6 How Often to Post New Content

Aside from the quality of your content, another factor Google takes into consideration is how updated your website is and how often new content is posted. As with almost everything else within Internet Marketing, there isn't a hard-and-fast rule about how frequently to post content.

Quality Versus Quantity

There are extremely successful people in this industry who only post once or twice a month. They focus on quality, so those one or two posts are the absolute best pieces of content on the topic they're writing about. The rest of their time is spent on promoting those few pieces of content.

Historically, **the more high-quality content you post, the better your odds are of getting rankings.** A good way to visualize this is to think about all the content you publish as digital shelf space you acquire with Google. In an actual grocery store, retailers want their goods to be seen by customers. The more goods they display on the grocery store shelves, the higher the chances that their goods will be bought by customers.

The same concept applies to your content: the more digital shelf space you acquire by having your content displayed in more SERPs, the more likely that internet users will see your content. Think of the first page of search results as the coveted eye-level shelf in a grocery store: the more content you can place there, the easier your content can be found by users.

My personal recommendation, which is what I do for new niche sites, is to **post at least two to three high-quality posts per week.**

Never Sacrifice Quality for Quantity

With that being said, if you can only get one really high-quality post out per week, go ahead and do that. Just because the ideal is twice or more per week doesn't mean you should skimp on the quality just to be able to put out content more frequently.

It also doesn't mean that you should give up. Go ahead and publish that high-quality post once a week. You'll take longer to achieve success than those who can publish two or three times a week, but you'll definitely get there. If your niche is competitive enough and you're selecting keywords well, doing on-page SEO just right, and your content is high-quality, you'll get there.

6.7 An Overview of High-Quality Content Creation

The working example we've been looking at up to this point is published on RueTattoo.com (*https:// ruetattoo.com/how-much-does-tattoo-removal-hurt/*). You can review the published post as you move through this section of Chapter 6.

Tips on Formatting Blog Posts

VERY Important Note: *Shortly before we published this book, Wordpress **dramatically** redesigned their visual page and post editor, so your screens won't quite match up with those in this book by default.*

You can switch back to Wordpress' "classic editor" very easily, which will make all of your screens when drafting pages or posts on your website match up with those within this book.

Just search the internet using a phrase along the lines of "how to change back to Wordpress classic editor" and you should be able to find multiple articles and videos that will walk you through this process step-by-step in less than five minutes.

Break up your paragraphs into smaller chunks. The following images show how overwhelming large paragraphs can be:

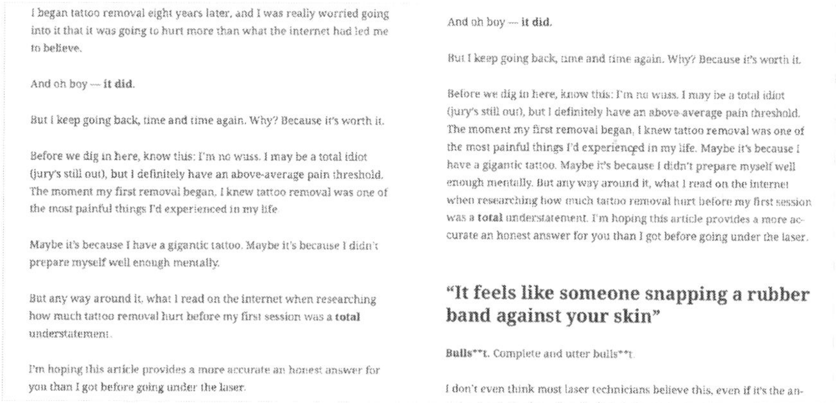

I began tattoo removal eight years later, and I was really worried going into it that it was going to hurt more than what the internet had led me to believe.

And oh boy — **it did.**

But I keep going back, time and time again. Why? Because it's worth it.

Before we dig in here, know this: I'm no wuss. I may be a total idiot (jury's still out), but I definitely have an above-average pain threshold. The moment my first removal began, I knew tattoo removal was one of the most painful things I'd experienced in my life

Maybe it's because I have a gigantic tattoo. Maybe it's because I didn't prepare myself well enough mentally.

But any way around it, what I read on the internet when researching how much tattoo removal hurt before my first session was a **total** understatement.

I'm hoping this article provides a more accurate an honest answer for you than I got before going under the laser.

And oh boy — **it did.**

But I keep going back, time and time again. Why? Because it's worth it.

Before we dig in here, know this: I'm no wuss. I may be a total idiot (jury's still out), but I definitely have an above-average pain threshold. The moment my first removal began, I knew tattoo removal was one of the most painful things I'd experienced in my life. Maybe it's because I have a gigantic tattoo. Maybe it's because I didn't prepare myself well enough mentally. But any way around it, what I read on the internet when researching how much tattoo removal hurt before my first session was a **total** understatement. I'm hoping this article provides a more accurate an honest answer for you than I got before going under the laser.

"It feels like someone snapping a rubber band against your skin"

Bulls**t. Complete and utter bulls**t.

I don't even think most laser technicians believe this, even if it's the an-

Fig. 06-09
Broken-up text (left) versus wall of text (right).

Note that the broken-up text on the left is much easier to read and digest than the larger paragraph on the right. Even if the text on the left consumes a larger area, the whitespace between each paragraph is a relief to the eyes.

Use headings and subheadings to create an organized structure. This makes it easier for the reader to skim your article and find the information they wish to read more thoroughly.

Tips on Adding Images to Blog Posts

Avoid inserting images directly above or below headers. Try to place images in between paragraphs or lines of text. You'll notice in the published post that I moved all images that were below headers or bullet points to areas in between paragraphs of text or removed them entirely when the bullet point was too short to justify the use of an image. **Don't feel the need to add images to every section**, particularly if the section is only a couple of sentences long.

If an image doesn't feel natural, don't force it. Sometimes an image breaks up the flow of text too much or just doesn't look right. Feel free to give up on using an image in these instances and opt for the next appropriate spot.

Don't spend too much time finding the perfect image. If you can't find the right image for your intended spot relatively quickly, just move on and come back to it at a later time.

Avoid using portrait-oriented images as much as possible because they leave too much awkward white space.

"It feels like someone snapping a rubber band against your skin"

Bulls**t. Complete and utter bulls**t.

I don't even think most laser technicians believe this, even if it's the answer they give when you ask them how much tattoo removal hurts.

This *might* be true if you can imagine someone snapping a rubber band against your skin several times per second, and sustaining that pace for 30-60 seconds (or more) at a time. But even that doesn't account for the heat.

"It feels like someone snapping a rubber band against your skin"

Bulls**t. Complete and utter bulls**t.

I don't even think most laser technicians believe this, even if it's the answer they give when you ask them how much tattoo removal hurts.

This *might* be true if you can imagine someone snapping a rubber band against your skin several times per second, and sustaining that pace for 30-60 seconds (or more) at a time. But even that doesn't account for the heat.

Tattoo removal feels like exactly what it is — a high-powered laser shooting deep into your skin and breaking up the pigment of your tattoo. That's not going to be a comfortable thing, no matter how you cut it.

If I had to compare it directly to tattoo application, I'd say it hurts 1.5x – 2x more than the most painful application spot during my tattoo — my sternum. So if you've ever had a sensitive, bony part of your body tat-

Fig. 06-10
Text with image (left) versus paragraphs of text (right).

Images do a great job of breaking up paragraphs of text. Even though these paragraphs aren't massive walls of text, it's still a good user experience to break up the monotony of text.

6.8 When to Expect Rankings

||||||||||||||||||||||||||||||||||||||||||||||||||||||||||||||||||||||||||||||||||||||||||||||||||||||

I've discussed the positive effects the right niche, the right keywords, and high-quality content have on keyword optimization. These elements all make it possible to get traffic and, eventually, rankings. After that, you should be able to start making money by providing affiliate offers and links within your content.

How Long Do I Have to Keep Doing This?

There are a lot of different moving parts, so there's no way to say for certain how long it will take to see the kind of traffic and rankings that bring you income. Some people may take four to six months to produce the same amount of quality work others may take 18 months to produce. There are many factors that decide how soon and to what degree someone will be successful in this industry, such as the niche and type of content.

How to Expedite the Process

The only thing I can say with complete certainty is that if you do the things that I've emphasized over and over again (choosing the right niche and keywords, writing optimized content around the right keywords, prioritizing value, etc.) you'll see results much faster than someone who isn't following what I've taught in this book.

But How Long Does *That* Take?

I've seen people make $2,000 or $3,000 a month within six to seven months of working in Internet Marketing. I've also seen people work diligently for 12 months with hardly any traffic to show for it.

The best I can do is give you an estimate:

 If you're posting high-quality content two to three times a week, you should start seeing results within the first eight to 12 months in a low-competition niche.

If you find yourself in a high-competition niche, make sure you're picking good keywords and not sacrificing quality to at least see some momentum building up in the first eight to 12 months.

After these eight to 12 months, start shifting your focus onto the aesthetics of your website, how well your website is converting, building an email list, and promoting your website. These are the things that are less important than your content but are nonetheless helpful to growing your website.

Some of you may think that you can tackle everything I've outlined in this book at the same time, but I beg to differ. From experience, focusing on one thing at a time ensures that you do that one thing well and that your website is built on an excellent foundation. Taking on several tasks at once makes your day more complicated. The more often this occurs, the higher the chances are that you're going to get overwhelmed and wash out. I want to prevent that as much as possible. I want to set you up for success and help change your life through an Internet Marketing business the same way I was able to change mine.

Focus on creating high-quality content for the first two to four months to practice these processes and to find the perfect rhythm that works for you and enables you to create content efficiently. When you're confident in your abilities, *then* you can take the next step in your Internet Marketing career, which is promoting your website to increase traffic.

Chapter 6 Summary

- High-quality content is an absolute must for any Internet Marketing business. The key to producing high-quality content is to focus on adding value to your followers' lives.

- If you are an incredible writer, everything will fall into place more quickly for you, but remember that you don't need to be perfect.

- When creating content, always think: "inch wide, mile deep."

- Every website needs a foundation of at least seven to 10 pieces of high-quality content before promotion.

- To prepare to write content you need to research and create an outline.

- Creating an outline helps you work more efficiently and thus accelerates the writing process. Aim to have an introduction, a conclusion, and a body with at least three main points.

- High-quality articles run between 1,200 to 1,500 words long.

- Never edit while writing and type drafts into a plain-text editor. Proofread and edit your work, apply the necessary formatting (e.g., emphasis on certain words, headlines, subheadlines, bullet points, etc.), and add relevant images only when you've moved your draft into WordPress.

- Break up your paragraphs into smaller chunks.

- Don't use stylish but hard-to-read fonts.

- Never justify the text on your articles.

- Aim to strike a balance between SEO and UX.

- Insert images throughout your article. Always determine if an image is copyrighted before using it on your website.

- My favorite image resources are: Pixabay.com, Unsplash.com, and Burst by Shopify.com.

- The most important aspects of your article to insert your keyword in are the post title, meta title, meta description, and URL slug.

- Use the keyword in one other subheader aside from your page title, in image alt tags when you can, and throughout your content where appropriate.

- The best SEO plugin for WordPress is Yoast SEO.

- If you're truly producing high-quality content around your focus keyword, you'll still manage to rank in Search Engine Result Pages (SERPs) even if you don't use the exact keyword often throughout the content.

- If you try and game Google's algorithms, your website will be penalized, resulting in lower rankings.

- The more high-quality content you post, the better your odds are of getting rankings.

- My own personal recommendation is to post at least two to three high-quality posts a week. When it comes to content, never sacrifice quality for quantity.

- Tips on Formatting Blog Posts:
  - Break up your paragraphs into smaller chunks.

- Use headings and subheadings to create an organized structure.

- Tips on Adding Images to Blog Posts:
  - Don't insert images directly above or below headers, if at all possible.
  - Don't feel the need to add images to every section.
  - If an image doesn't feel natural, don't force it.
  - Don't spend too much time finding the perfect image.
  - As much as possible, don't use portrait-oriented images.

- Focus on creating high-quality content and providing value to your readers, and you'll eventually achieve success. If you're posting high-quality content two to three times a week, you should start seeing momentum build up within the first eight to 12 months.

- How long it takes to rank in SERPs will vary based on the niche and the competition.

CHAPTER 6 SUMMARY

Chapter 7: How to Promote Your Website and Get Traffic

Writing high-quality content and optimizing it for search engines isn't the only way to get traffic. This chapter is dedicated to sharing promotion techniques for your website.

Keep in mind: **only posting high-quality content consistently is enough to succeed in any niche.** However, if doing nothing but working on content drives you nuts, I'd recommend picking ONE other form of promotion taught in this chapter to grow your business.

You only need one core competency plus one way to generate traffic to build a highly profitable internet business. Anything beyond that will likely lead to confusion and being overwhelmed, and, ultimately, increase the odds of giving up on your internet business.

7.1 "Post and Pray" Method: The Simplest Time-Tested Path to Success

The "Post and Pray" method, as I like to call it, is basically everything covered in the previous chapters; namely, identifying keywords, crafting high-quality content around those keywords, and optimizing content for search engines.

This technique is much maligned in the industry. Honestly, it's the simplest, time-tested, lowest cost, and penalty-proof way to build a sustainable authoritative brand in whatever niche you're aiming to establish yourself in. As a matter of fact, I've successfully built several businesses in this industry using the "Post and Pray" method.

I'm a huge proponent of this method because I believe people like simplicity. It's like spinning plates: the more plates you add at a single time, the more complicated the technique gets, and the more likely everything will come crashing down.

Even Google has specifically stated that this is the best way to build an authority website. As long as you have the patience to do it right and not game the system, you shouldn't have to worry about penalties. Simply post content consistently and you'll move steadily up the rankings.

I really like this method, but I want to make sure that I'm enabling you to explore other ways to promote your website and point you in the right direction. Done correctly, you can potentially see results much faster than you would from consistently posting high-quality content. Always remember not to overwhelm yourself by learning too many techniques, though.

7.2 Social Media (For What It's Worth)

IIIIIIIIIIIIIIIIIIIIIIIIIIIIIIIIIIIIIIIIIIIIIIIIIIIIIIIIIIIIIIIIIIIIIIIIIIIIIIIIIIIIIIIIIIIIIIIIII

What I'm going to say about social media contradicts what other people in the industry have said.

To be honest, **I hate social media for my websites.**

I hate the process of writing a post, taking it over to Facebook, Twitter, Google+, Instagram, Snapchat, and Pinterest, and who knows where else. I have to create different-sized images for each of these networks and write catchy taglines to entice people to click to get to my website.

For me, that's a lot of time I could be spending on my business and doing things that are going to make me more money, such as finding new keywords, writing more content, and optimizing that content.

This opinion may contradict what other marketers say about social media, social proof, and social signals. However, I've had websites raking in five figures monthly that have no social media presence; no Facebook page, Twitter, or Instagram account. Don't get me wrong: there is value to social media. For the vast majority of niche sites that other people are building in this industry, though, it's unnecessary and can be a waste of time.

I *will* concede that for some niches it makes a lot of sense to integrate social media. For those niches, the emphasis is placed on making content viral for engagement (commenting, sharing, and tagging friends).

I recommend figuring out if social media is indeed a good fit for you and your content. More often than not, though, your time is probably better spent focusing on SEO, improving your writing skills, or interacting with influencers in your industry.

Who SHOULD Pursue Social Media

Those who are trying to build lifestyle-based brands would have the most to gain from social media. These are the niches that benefit from sleek and stylish photos because they involve building a very specific persona that can only be accurately conveyed through high-quality images and videos. Examples of niches social media works well for are supplements, beauty, or fashion.

If you have a knack for social media and enjoy it, there are plenty of marketers who teach those techniques really well. Unfortunately, I'm not one of them. So, if social media is something you absolutely want to pursue, then the best advice I can give is to find *where* your target audience is. For example, if your audience is younger, they're more likely on Instagram and Snapchat rather than Facebook.

Who Should NOT Pursue Social Media

I'm giving permission to anyone who finds social media too intimidating to say, "screw it," and spend their time in other productive ways.

Focus on things you know you can do well, don't overwhelm you, and don't feel like an inefficient use of time. If you think you should be focusing on learning how to research better keywords or how to write better content, do that instead! More high-quality content translates to more money.

Where to Learn More About Social Media

If I can't provide the absolute best training, I'm not going to teach it. What I will do is direct you to those who do. I recommend researching "social media marketing guide" in Google to find several experts that can train you in the ways of social media.

Companies that specialize in software for social media, such as HootSuite and Buffer, have excellent blogs and resources with helpful tips and tricks. I would follow their advice when it comes to social media matters.

Again, I'm really not the best person to teach you about social media, but I am the best example

7.2 SOCIAL MEDIA (FOR WHAT IT'S WORTH)

of an Internet Marketer who doesn't like social media and almost never uses it but achieved success anyway.

7.3 Video Marketing

Video Marketing is one of my favorite ways to crack high-competition niches. You get to leverage the Domain Authority of YouTube, which is a perfect 100 on a scale from one to 100. Plus, you can also receive traffic through the "Suggested Videos" feature of YouTube.

The Most Enduring Myth About Video Marketing

A myth about Video Marketing is that you need excellent editing skills to tap into it. People believe that for a video to be successful, it needs flashy graphics and transitions. **That's just not true.**

My early Video Marketing years were absolutely atrocious: low-quality lighting with horrible audio from a crappy built-in microphone on a crappy webcam with no noise-canceling, so my ceiling fan can be heard spinning. My videos have come so far from those days.

You probably won't have that bad of a start, but the point is that you'll get better over time, no matter how crappy you think your initial setup is.

What You Need to Get Started

For a setup that's better than 80% to 90% of what's on YouTube, all you really need is three-point lighting (one on either side of the camera and one at the back of the subject), a decent lapel or lavalier microphone, and a high-quality, high-definition web camera.

These days, this equipment is affordable and easy to acquire. Even mid-level smartphones include good high-definition cameras. A decent lapel microphone on Amazon can cost less than $30, and three-point lighting can be set up with desk lamps you may already have in your home.

Another thing you need to be successful in Internet Marketing is patience: patience to consistently produce video content, and the patience to practice and be comfortable in front of the camera.

How to Supplement Written Content with Video

A written post can be supplemented with a corresponding video. So, instead of creating three or four posts a week, you can create two posts plus two videos each week.

In time, people who browse videos on YouTube will start finding your videos. Those who are interested in your videos will go to your website and read your other content, increasing traffic to your website. An advantage of adding video content to your catalog is that you double your reach and therefore increase the possibility of attaining success sooner.

YouTube SEO is very similar to SEO for your written content. Start with keyword research and make sure that ones you select are in the video title, description, and tags. If you embed your video in a related post on your website, as that post gains authority with search engines, your embedded video will also gain authority within YouTube.

Where to Learn More About Video Content

A great resource is the article *Do Your YouTube Videos Suck? Make Them High Quality Using These 4 Simple Tips* on *Entrepreneur.com*, which is a guide to making high-quality videos. Alternatively, you can always find quality articles by doing a Google search.

7.4 Automated Traffic and Traffic Networks

IIIIIIIIIIIIIIIIIIIIIIIIIIIIIIIIIIIIIIIIIIIIIIIIIIIIIIIIIIIIIIIIIIIIIIIIIIIIIIIIIIIIIIIIIIIIIIIIIIIIIIIIIIIIIIIIIII

I get asked about automated traffic and traffic networks all the time by newbies in this industry, and my answer is always the same: **don't use them.**

What is Automated Traffic?

Automated traffic is purchased traffic that someone has sent to your website via robots that spike your website statistics and make your analytics look good. These robots also try to make the traffic look as natural and organic as possible by clicking a few pages on your site and lingering for a while.

Why is Automated Traffic a Bad Idea?

Any engagement that's purchased, such as purchased social media likes or video views on YouTube, are a total waste of time. This type of engagement is sold by salespeople who make outrageous and false claims.

There are no shortcuts to making money online. Buying a thousand visitors a day to your site and consequently making 10 to 20 grand a month doesn't happen. It just doesn't work that way.

Not only does bought engagement not work, there's a real possibility that your business will suffer. It takes away your focus from doing things that are *actually* beneficial to your website, like better keyword research and content.

It's worth noting that Google, and other search engines, sometimes penalize sites and even remove them from their indexes so the pages aren't displayed anymore because of bought engagement. They've done this to many websites in the past, and I'd hate for that to happen to you.

7.5 A Brief Discussion About Paid Traffic

Paid traffic is any traffic to your website that you paid to obtain. Some common forms of paid traffic are Pay Per View and Pay Per Click (PPC) on YouTube, Google, Bing, Yahoo!, or Facebook. Strictly speaking, it also includes Direct Mail and Media Buys (TV or radio space).

There don't seem to be any courses that truly teach paid traffic well. I recommend a book by Brad Geddes called *Advanced Google AdWords* (the latest edition) if you want to learn more about paid traffic.

The good thing about PPC Marketing in particular is that when you build a particularly profitable group of PPC ads (called a campaign), you can ramp up from making $100 profit a day to making $1,000 to $2,000 profit a day (maybe even $3,000 on a good day) in the span of a week.

The bad thing about PPC is that you need to spend a lot of money, time, and effort to reach that point. Plus, people who can afford spying tools are able to check on your campaign. When they see that it's profitable, they can underbid you and build out funnels that have higher lifetime value for their visitors than your campaign does. In the end, you'll get pushed out of the market you cornered.

Who SHOULD Pursue Paid Traffic

Some aspiring Internet Marketers think spending $5 a day for a couple of months and then scaling up a campaign will make them rich. Sorry to say the game doesn't work that way. Believe me, *I know*. I used to do this myself when I started out in Affiliate Marketing, and I learned my lesson the hard (and expensive) way.

 The people who should pursue paid traffic are those with thick skin and plenty of money to burn. I'm talking $2,000 and up while you're learning the ropes. Pursuing paid traffic requires money to pay for a ton of data that needs interpreting, and, based on those interpretations, the ads and landing pages you'll need to tweak. You can drop hundreds and thousands of dollars just to have access to that data. By the time you've built up a profitable campaign, you may have dropped thousands of dollars into it.

Pursuing paid traffic also requires thick skin to avoid the panic that comes from the fact that spending thousands of dollars of your money without breaking even is a very real possibility. You need the patience to learn how to make it work, pore over spreadsheets of data, fine tune your ads and/or landing pages, and then try again. This cycle can go on for weeks before a campaign becomes profitable. The important thing is to stay level-headed throughout all the learning and tweaking and interpreting.

Who Should NOT Pursue Paid Traffic

The people who shouldn't pursue paid traffic are those who are looking for low-cost and relatively easy methods of getting traffic. Some people have misconceptions that paid traffic is an easy way to get qualified traffic to their site, and they couldn't be more wrong. Qualified traffic takes money, time, effort, research, crunching numbers, analyzing data, looking at spreadsheets, and analytical skills.

My PPC Story

My latest PPC site was an ecommerce site that was earning $100,000 or more a month in revenue. That translated to around $25,000 to $30,000 a month in profit because I was spending $20,000 to $30,000 a month on Facebook advertising.

It fizzled.

The success from the site came and went in the span of four months because the competition increased to the point that I got pushed out of the industry. Nevertheless, I'm currently testing new methods and trying to crack back into the profitable side of that niche.

Nothing compares to the rush of raking in the profits. At the same time, that success can be swept right out from under you.

7.6 Other Excellent Resources

At this point, if you're comfortable with taking on a bit more complexity and feel that you can handle adding promotion to your SEO strategy to get traffic to your site, I'd like to share some excellent resources and further reading.

Before I proceed, though, I'd like to remind you that if this is your first time in Internet Marketing, and you haven't had a profitable website before, keeping things simple will increase your chances of sticking with it and achieving success.

Expert Roundups

An Expert Roundup involves sending a provocative or interesting question about a topic to other experts in your industry whose answers you include in an article. The idea is for these experts to share your content with their followers when you notify them that their answers were included in your content.

This practice helps form relationships with other experts in your industry and get on their radar for future partnerships, guest blogging, and other collaborations.

Expert roundups are a good way to start seeing traction a lot faster, especially if you hold one every month, because when you quote an expert, they will often share your post with *their* followers. Experts usually have thousands of followers on social media. Needless to say, that's a lot of people who are going to see your content and likely click your link.

It's wise to already have at least five to 10 high-quality posts by the time you start doing Expert Roundups, though. When their followers come to your website, the last thing you want them to see is a bare website. You want to come across as an authority so that when visitors read your articles, they'll want to read more.

SmartBlogger.com published a comprehensive and tremendously helpful step-by-step guide to creating expert roundups titled *The Ultimate Guide to Creating an Expert Roundup Post That Gets 1000s of Shares*.

Off-Page SEO

Off-page SEO centers around getting high-quality links to pages you're trying to rank. I've discussed on-page SEO, but off-page SEO also plays an important role in whether or not you get rankings. I'd even venture to say that while on-page SEO is the foundation, off-page SEO is where the battle is won. If you don't pay attention and do a sloppy job, you run the risk of rendering your website useless.

If off-page SEO sounds right up your alley, then I HIGHLY recommend *The Ultimate Guide to Off-Page SEO* by Neil Patel found on *NeilPatel.com*.

Guest Blogging

Guest blogging involves writing a blog post and having it published on another website. Use the relationships you've formed from expert roundups to score guest blogging opportunities.

The goal here is to get your content in front of a new audience, as well as linking to your website from a website that has more authority. In that respect, guest blogging can be considered a form of off-page SEO.

If guest blogging sounds like something you'd like to do, the article *Guest Blogging: The Definitive Guide (2018)* on *Backlinko.com* walks you through guest blogging, step-by-step.

60 Free Traffic Strategies

If none of the former options sound good to you, or you'd like to know other ways to promote your website, I have an in-depth article on Stopping Scams titled *60 Ways To Promote Your Blog: Free Traffic Strategies That Work* that lists 60 free ways to promote your blog.

The list may seem overwhelming (the article itself is almost 15,000 words long) but remember: **you don't have to do them all**. I recommend browsing through the ideas and picking two or three that you can comfortably do in conjunction with creating high-quality content for your website.

Try one of these promotion strategies for a month or two and see if your website is gaining traction. If there isn't much traction after that period, then you may need to stick with that strategy a while longer or choose another one from the list. Regardless of what you do, never neglect the quality of your content. That should always take priority over promotion.

Chapter 7 Summary

|||||||||||||||||||||||||||||||||||||||||||||||||||||||||||||||||||||||||||||||||||||||||||||||||||||||||

- The "Post and Pray" method involves identifying keywords, crafting high-quality content around those keywords, optimizing content for search engines, and repeating those steps for different keywords until your website gathers a collection of high-quality content and builds authority.

- I recommend determining if social media is a good fit for you and your content. Those who are trying to build lifestyle-based brands would have the most to gain from social media.

- For visual media, all you need is three-point lighting (one on either side of the camera and one at the back), a decent lapel or lavalier microphone, and a high-quality, high-definition web camera.

- Don't buy automated traffic. At best, they're a waste of time. At the worst, you can end up sabotaging your own website.

- The people who should pursue paid traffic (e.g., pay per click (PPC) on Google) are those who have thick skin and plenty of money to burn.

- Excellent Resources:

  - *The Ultimate Guide to Creating an Expert Roundup Post That Gets 1000s of Shares – SmartBlogger.com*

  - *The Ultimate Guide to Off-Page SEO – NeilPatel.com*

  - *Guest Blogging: The Definitive Guide (2018) – Backlinko.com*

  - *60 Ways To Promote Your Blog: Free Traffic Strategies That Work – StoppingScams. com*

Chapter 8: Now How Do I Make Money?

Up until now I've spent a fair share of this training focusing on one thing: how to get traffic.

But after you get traffic, **how do you make money?**

That's what this chapter is dedicated to. From CPA Marketing to selling your own physical products, you'll learn about all of the monetization options.

8.1 When and How to Monetize Your Content
|||||||||||||||||||||||||||||||||||||||||||||||||||||||||||||||||||||||||||||||||||||||||||||||||||||||||||||

You didn't spend all that time and effort building a website, creating high-quality content, optimizing for search engines, and establishing your authority for nothing. There will come a time to monetize your content.

However, remember that you don't need to concern yourself with monetization until you're getting consistent traffic.

When Can I Start Monetizing My Content?

You might have noticed that when I posted my first article on *RueTattoo.com*, I didn't add any affiliate links or calls to action. In my experience, spending time on that is pointless until you start seeing which posts are getting the most traffic and engagement.

For one thing, I could spend at least a few hours hunting down affiliate offers to fit into that content. Additionally, I could spend a few more hours creating the right lead magnet to convince people to opt in to my email list.

If I spent my time doing this for a single article, publishing two articles a week, then my time is going into articles that I'm not even sure will gain traction. That's time that could have gone towards traffic-producing activities, like creating content and promoting my site.

 Once you're consistently getting 75 to 100 visitors a day, it's time to start getting serious about monetization.

At that point, you'll know which posts are consistently receiving a lot of traffic, and you can focus monetization efforts on those posts instead of all of them. This strategy will get you better results.

75 to 100 visitors a day doesn't translate to a full-time income in most niches, but it's at this point

you need to at least start optimizing your posts to make money. Some of the options you have for monetization include advertising, Cost Per Acquisition (CPA) Marketing, or dropshipping and selling your own physical or digital products.

Advertising

Advertising is one of the most straightforward and easy to implement methods of monetization, especially with Google AdSense. It's as easy as copying a code from Google AdSense, pasting it on your website, and automatically populating your designated space with ads. You then get paid based on how many times people click those ads on your website.

However, advertising doesn't make a lot of sense unless you're receiving a lot of traffic. In Chapter 1 we did some reverse math and computed that you'd need hundreds of thousands, if not millions, of visitors a month to get a decent income from advertising. Unfortunately, the vast majority of websites never make it to that level of traffic volume.

Cost Per Acquisition (CPA) Marketing

CPA is a pricing model that involves the advertiser paying for a particular acquisition, such as a sale (pay-per-sale), click (pay-per-click), form submission (pay-per-lead), or any other measurable action. There are several CPA networks that have all kinds of offers to compare and shop for. What you need to do is get an affiliate link so the advertisers can track the clicks and actions from your website.

It's best to integrate CPA offers in your content with buttons throughout the post. This can be done by adding a button with a compelling call to action at some point in your content that not only ties contextually into the content but is also really enticing for the reader to click. Do this at multiple points throughout the article.

Another way to integrate CPA offers in your content is through in-text links. Again, find points in the post where you can insert links that are contextually related. In my experience, affiliate links that are integrated with the content convert much better. Visitors are more curious, and therefore more likely to click, about links if they're relevant and appear *while* they're reading. Placing your affiliate links in banners and sidebars doesn't attract as many clicks; people have been trained to almost ignore sidebars and banners because they're expected to be ads.

Just remember that when it comes to sharing affiliate links, you are legally required to make it explicit. Some marketers try to bury this disclaimer in their terms and conditions, but that's not just frowned upon; there can be real legal consequences. I would advise that you familiarize yourself with any laws that your country may have regarding advertising and affiliate links.

Rather than see this transparency as a hindrance, I see it as a great way to forge trust in my relationship with my audience. Personally, I make my affiliate links absolutely clear with disclaimers, like the following:

> *"This is an affiliate link. This is how we stay funded and these commissions are what keep our site going. Please support us by purchasing through our affiliate link."*

Believe it or not, disclaimers like this are a highly compelling way to increase conversions because when you're truly promoting things that are valuable to your audience, there's no reason for them not to support you and purchase through your affiliate link. If you've really gone out of your way to create high-quality content that brings value to their life, and they're going to have to pay the same amount or less elsewhere, they might as well click your link to show their support.

 You can find many CPA offers through sites like *OfferVault.com* and *Affplus.com* no matter what your niche is. You can also read reviews from more established affiliates on *Affpaying.com* so you know which CPA networks are worth your time.

Note whether the advertisers stiff people on commissions, how helpful the affiliate managers are, how great the offer selection is, and how the payouts compare to other CPA networks. While you can have more than one CPA offer on your site, try not to push them all in a single post.

Once you've selected a CPA network to apply for, next make sure you're getting enough visitors so that you're more likely to get approved. CPA networks don't normally approve brand new websites unless the owner has been in touch with an affiliate manager and shown that they're trustworthy and know what they're talking about.

Physical Products That You Own vs. Dropshipping

Dropshipping is a method of monetization that involves a seller purchasing the item from a third party and having it shipped to the customer. In this setup, the seller never sees or handles the product. If you decide to go this route, consider expanding into managing your own inventory and sourcing your own products as the volume increases.

 The go-to site for low-cost products is *AliExpress.com*, an online marketplace where small businesses in China offer products to international online buyers. When sourcing products from

AliExpress.com, the ideal thing to do is to order the product first and verify the quality. If you can't do this, at least make sure to research your suppliers thoroughly: read the reviews, how many purchases they've handled, and how many times the product you want to offer has been sold. Otherwise, you can end up shipping a total piece of crap to your customer, which is going to hurt your reputation and relationship with your subscribers.

I discuss how to sell products via dropshipping in an article titled *How to Make Money Dropshipping Using AliExpress and Shopify*, along with my personal dropshipping experiences, on *StoppingScams.com*. If you're interested in this route, check out the article.

The usual conversion rate when selling physical products ranges from 0.5% to 1%. When you're starting to gain traction and only getting 75 to 100 visitors a day, that means you sell 1 product every day. With dropshipping, you minimize the overhead costs while being able to mark up the products at least two to three times.

Most of the suppliers at *AliExpress.com* aren't the manufacturers; they're middlemen who buy the products in bulk (hundreds or thousands of units at a time) and mark them up. When your traffic increases so you can move more products in a day, you can venture into sourcing or manufacturing your own products.

Once your site receives the number of orders to justify buying in bulk, you can go straight to the manufacturer and cut your cost per item while maintaining your selling price. This means you get to keep more of the profit. If you can afford the equipment, you can go straight to manufacturing the products yourself. Sourcing or manufacturing products would be more expensive due to the overhead costs, but the higher profit margins, plus greater control over the quality of the products, make it worthwhile to pursue. This is an often overlooked way to monetize a website.

For example, a person may start a beer brewing website and try to monetize it by creating a digital product or affiliating with other information products. With enough traffic, they could dropship their own brewing supplies from China directly to customers. Over time and with more customers, they could start building their own brand and source or manufacture products with their brand name and logo.

Digital Products

Digital products are products that are stored, delivered, and consumed in an electronic format. These include books, digital images, stock photos, digital videos, e-courses, software, audio files, and any other item that is stored as a file.

Typically, people don't start by releasing their own digital product. Much like selling physical products, you test the waters with a similar affiliate offer first. Once the traffic is generated and the perfect sales funnel is in place, then you can spend time creating a digital product.

If you're interested in creating a digital product, I recommend waiting until you're receiving at least 200 to 300 visitors a day. Personally, I'd be comfortable with at least 700 to 1,000 visitors per day. At that point, if you've tested the waters with CPA marketing, it's wise to do in-depth market research to find out what your audience is really interested in. Email subscribers and ask what their biggest concerns are. Then, start building your product around those struggles and pain points.

Putting together a high quality digital product is probably going to take at least a few weeks of full-time work, so it's crucial that you do your market research thoroughly before starting.

As with physical products, your reputation and your brand are on the line. If followers of your website buy something from you and it's not the quality that they've come to expect, they're unlikely to trust your future products. Once that trust is gone, that bridge is burned along with any future opportunity to make money from that customer.

Value Ladders

With digital products, you can build a **value ladder**, which is a method of mapping out your product offerings in ascending order of value and price. This way, you can cater to your customers in whatever stage they're at.

For example, if your niche is photography, start with a free lead magnet of five high-quality stock photos in exchange for subscribing to your mailing list. Then, start selling a bundle of 20 high-quality stock photos for $1 and make sure the quality of the photos is evident. After that, upsell a $47 course on how to take high-quality photographs so the customer never has to buy stock photography again. The next level could be an upsell to a $100 a month membership to ongoing courses and coaching. Beyond that, you can offer a super high-quality course for $1,000 to $2,000 on how to start a local photography business.

Typically, you tend to over deliver to the point of losing money at the bottom of your value ladder. This is not self-sabotage; it's to establish that you are trustworthy and credible. As your customers move up the value ladder, you progressively make more money per customer while delivering more value to them.

Conversion Rate Optimization: The Basics

It's not enough to be able to monetize your traffic. It's more important to be able to convert the traffic you *do* get into subscribers and customers. To do this, you have to be able to test different elements of your website and tweak them so that more of your visitors feel inclined to do what you're guiding them to do. That, in a nutshell, is conversion rate optimization.

Many people place ads on their site or free lead magnets along with other offers (such as physical or digital products) to entice visitors to join their mailing list. **Increasing the number of different elements on the page actually decreases the chances that visitors will click on any of the offers.** What you're doing is pulling someone in multiple directions. It's been shown that when people are given too many options, they just don't make a decision.

The best thing to do here is to design individual posts and pages so that all of the page elements (sidebars, banners, in-text links, calls to action) lead visitors to a single action. This action could be downloading a free whitepaper, buying from one of your affiliates, or buying a video course in exchange for joining your mailing list. It doesn't matter what the offer is, as long as it's relevant to the content and it's a single target.

For example, in *StoppingScams.com*, when a post is about Internet Marketing, I only pitch Internet Marketing. When a post is about surveys, I only pitch surveys; I don't mix and match.

The most important thing to remember here is to only integrate offers that are actually valuable to your audience. If you're writing a piece of content about a specific topic or about how to solve a pain point, pitch things that are actually valuable and helpful to your audience. Don't pitch a product you believe will make you the most money because if it isn't relevant to what they're reading, your visitors won't be interested in clicking, and that's going to decrease your conversion rate. By only pitching relevant and helpful offers, you help forge a relationship that you can continue to monetize over time.

In terms of dollars, it's better to pitch a relevant offer that makes you $10 rather than an irrelevant offer that makes you $100. If the $10 offer is truly valuable and helpful, more visitors will convert, and you can potentially make up the difference.

The first time you recommend something that's not relevant or useful to your visitors, trust is broken, and you can consider that relationship over.

8.2 STOP HERE (Until You're Getting Consistent Traffic)

IIIIIIIIIIIIIIIIIIIIIIIIIIIIIIIIIIIIIIIIIIIIIIIIIIIIIIIIIIIIIIIIIIIIIIIIIIIIIIIIIIIIIIIIIIIIIIIIIIIIIIIII

I know it may not feel like it, but it's time to stop and focus on getting traffic.

Why It's Time to Stop (For Now)

There is still so much to learn, and your instinct may be to want to keep learning.

Right now, you have everything you need to get traffic. From doing keyword research, to writing high-quality content, to incorporating one method of promotion, all these steps are going to move traffic to your site as long as you stick with the process. Focusing on other things will unnecessarily complicate things.

If you worry about how perfect the aesthetics on your website are, you have to think about the design. You need to incorporate your banner so that visitors can opt-in to your email list, which means you need to learn how an autoresponder works. Then, you need to come up with an email sequence, which means you need to learn how to write sales copy and how to convert people through an email list and how to nurture a relationship through email marketing. Then, you have to figure out how to increase your conversions.

Some of you who are beginners may have read the previous paragraph like it was gibberish, and that's a perfectly reasonable reaction. That's how quickly thinking about other things besides traffic can get out of control. At this time, focus on doing killer keyword research, putting out high-quality content, promoting that content, and doing it all over again to get traffic, gain traction, and build the authority of your website.

It's **truly** all you need to create a profitable online business using less than $100 starting capital and **a lot** of consistent hard work.

Chapter 8 Summary

||||||||||||||||||||||||||||||||||||||||||||||||||||||||||||||||||||||||||||||||||||||||||||||||||||||||||||

- Think about monetization once your website gets 75 to 100 visitors a day.

- Advertising is the easiest monetization method to implement, but it just isn't a good idea unless you have traffic in the hundreds of thousands or millions of visitors a month.

- CPA is a pricing model where the advertiser pays for a particular acquisition, such as a sale (pay-per-sale), click (pay-per-click), form submission (pay-per-lead), or any other measurable action.

- Dropshipping is a method wherein a seller doesn't keep the products in stock; instead, the seller purchases their goods from a third party and has them shipped to the customer. This way, the seller never sees or handles the product.

- When selling physical products, you can go from offering them through affiliate links, to dropshipping them, to actually manufacturing or sourcing them.

- Digital products are the hardest and longest to create, but through value ladders, can be the most profitable of them all.

- The first time you recommend something that's not relevant or useful to your visitors, subscribers, or customers, trust is broken and you can consider that relationship over.

- Increasing the number of different elements on a page actually decreases the chances that visitors will click on any of the offers.

- The best thing to do is wash, rinse, repeat: do killer keyword research, put out high-quality content, and promote your content until you get consistent traffic.

- After you get consistent traffic, that's when you can think about all the other aspects of

CHAPTER 8 SUMMARY

Internet Marketing (e.g., website design, email marketing, conversion optimization, sales copywriting).

Final Thoughts: Focus On Becoming the PERSON Who Can Achieve Your Dreams

If there's one thing this training emphasizes, it's that there's more to Internet Marketing than a lot of product publishers would have you believe. Learning and understanding is only the beginning.

An Iron Mindset is the key to your success on this journey. That's what makes the difference between those who succeed, and those who fail in this industry.

When you feel stuck, burnt out, or that you've lost focus, remember the three main factors of the Iron Mindset to help you get back on track: be extremely determined, understand that this is a non-linear journey, and never give up.

This is the advice I wish someone had given me at the very beginning of my entrepreneurial journey because it took nearly 10 years to figure out on my own:

The only way to fail in this industry is if you give up.

My goals and dreams have always been ambitious. When I first started in Internet Marketing,

I didn't have the discipline to reach my potential, so achieving those dreams was always a struggle.

The reason I was finally able to gain traction is because I actively shifted my mindset. I knew that in order to achieve the level of success I aimed for I would have to invest time and effort to become more disciplined.

Goal setting can be difficult; acting on those goals can be even more challenging. If you're struggling to get started, I encourage you to research an individual who has reached or achieved the goals you've set, then emulate their behavior. Study that person's patterns and habits, then start practicing them.

When you practice something new for several weeks it eventually becomes habitual. Be careful, though - the last thing you want is to burn yourself out before you even get started.

Adopting several new habits at the same time is not a great way to set yourself up for success because doing several things at once is overwhelming. Eventually you'll blame yourself for washing out and not being as successful as you wanted to be **because you attempted too much at once.**

Don't fall into the trap of attempting to read a book per week while also integrating a new exercise and sleep routine all at once. **You'll overwhelm yourself.**

Instead, focus on adopting one new habit for several weeks, and only worry about introducing another once you've successfully mastered the first. This is the best way to form the habits of the person you're emulating.

Along with everything else I discuss in FIMP regarding goal setting and mindset, focus on becoming the **person** who can achieve your dreams. Ask yourself, *"How dedicated am I willing to be in order to achieve success?"*

The level of success you achieve is in your control. There will be many, many times you'll want to give up because you'll be overworked, overwhelmed, and tired. To be successful in the Internet Marketing industry, you'll need to overcome those feelings.

Always remember that the **only** way anyone's journey stops in this industry...

...is if they give up.

About Ian Pribyl

Ian Pribyl began his journey into online business at just 16 years old. Even from that age, he recognized internet business as a path to complete independence in life, geography, and business.

Fast-forward 15 years, and he's been a top-ranked super affiliate for multiple companies around

the world, created and operated e-commerce stores with six-figure monthly revenues, and currently runs all marketing for a startup he co-founded in the optometric & optical industries.

Ian is also the Founder of *First-Time Internet Marketing Profits™ (FIMP)*, the video training that this book is derived from, where he spends his spare time adding new video content and regularly supporting his community.

He continues his mission to help others achieve complete independence through internet business, the same way he did many years ago, while living with his wife and three miniature dachshunds in Austin, Texas.

Published in March 2019
by Ian Pribyl

ian@StoppingScams.com